Learn English This Way

10 Lessons from Beginner to Intermediate Level

The ESL Workbook for Adults

Larisa Tazmin

Table of Contents

Text: **Today and Yesterday**

Affirmatives, negatives, and questions with the helping verb **did**:

- I/You/She/He/It/We/They + verb (past form)…
- I/You/She/He/It/We/They **didn't** (did not) + verb…
- **Did** I/you/she/he/it/we/they + verb…?
- What **did** I/you/she/he/it/we/they + verb…?

Verbs: the Past Simple tense

Simple sentences ➜ compound and complex sentences

Adjectives ➜ adverbs

Words—letters—sounds: **y**esterday—"y"—/j/; thi**ng**/tha**n**k—"ng" "n"—/ŋ/; **j**oke—"j"—/dʒ/

Text: **Today and Tomorrow**

Affirmatives, negatives, and questions with the helping verb **will**:

- I/You/She/He/It/We/They **will** + verb…
- I/You/She/He/It/We/They **won't** (will not) + verb…
- **Will** I/you/she/he/it/we/they + verb…?
- What **will** I/you/she/he/it/we/they + verb…?

Verbs: the Future Simple tense

Simple sentences ➜ conditional sentences

Adjectives/adverbs: comparatives—superlatives: good/well—better—best

Words—letters—sounds: wi**ll**—"ll"—/ɫ/; be**tt**er/wa**t**er—"tt" "t"—/t̬/; impor**tan**t—"tan"—/ʔn̩/; li**sten**—"sten"—/sn/

Text: **About me**

Affirmatives, negatives, and questions with the present forms of the verb **be**:

- I **am**…/am doing…
- She/He/It **is**…/is doing…
- You/We/They **are**…/are doing…

Tag questions: You're a student, aren't you?

Verbs: the Present Progressive tense/Present passive voice

Present participle: verb + ing: asking, doing, going, writing, greeting

Past participle: verb + ed: asked, greeted

Future forms: do/will do/be + doing/be going + to do

Pronouns: possessive/reflexive: mine, my own, myself

Pronunciation: contractions, reductions

Introduction

There are plenty of ESL books and websites waiting for you to start learning English. Most of them begin with the alphabet and the verb "to be." The student's mind picks up the pattern "I am…" and often doesn't let it go. Then "am" is used where it's not needed.

If you're a complete beginner and don't know the English letters, you can easily familiarize yourself with the alphabet. You don't need a book to teach you the English letters when they are all around!

This course doesn't begin with the English alphabet and the verb "to be." It offers a different yet simple and sensible approach to ESL learning. It can help you start or restart your English studies on your own and/or with an English teacher.

What is the methodology in this workbook?

The workbook contains 10 extensive lessons, each one averaging out to ten pages. They together cover all the necessary language material to move you to the intermediate level.

The lessons are centered around the three important English verbs in the sequence of Do → Be → Have. They are built from easy to difficult. First, the target (selected) language material is introduced in contexts (different forms of speech) for awareness. Then it is isolated for focused learning in tasks of different complexity. This work gradually leads you to using the language material in your own speech. You should use a pencil and perform the exercises in the workbook itself.

This book teaches all three aspects of the language: pronunciation, grammar, and vocabulary with the help of the symbols (→), tables, brief instructions, prompts, and examples.

All four speech activities are involved, in the following succession: listening/silent reading → writing/reading out loud → speaking. Listening, reading, and writing are the basis of speaking. Writing precedes and improves speaking.

The first six lessons give weight to phonetics (sounds) as pronunciation is important for confident communication in spoken English, so it should be practiced from the very beginning. The last four lessons integrate pronunciation within the language material. The pronunciation is based on American English.

How to use this workbook?

You need to use a dictionary or online translator whenever necessary, especially for the instructions on how to do the exercises. Here is how to approach each lesson:

1. Note what you are going to learn in each lesson. A lesson overview is provided before the lesson begins.
2. Follow the exact sequence of the lesson. It starts with the introductory text for listening and silent reading. (All introductory texts are recorded and available on the YouTube channel "Learn English This Way" with a video for each lesson. You can search, for example: Learn English This Way: Lesson 1.)
3. Listen to and read the text silently. The text is the input. It demonstrates the use of the selected language in different kinds of contexts: instructions, stories, conversations, and descriptions. The text is accompanied by a list of the words found in the text. They should be looked up in the dictionary (translated). Later, some vocabulary is explained through synonyms and comments.
4. Move on to the sentence level where the target grammar is taken out of the context and presented in sentences for illustration and practice.
5. Move on to the level of words. At this stage, particular words are taken from the sentences for learning, reading, and pronunciation.
6. Practice pronunciation of the target (specific) sounds individually and in words. After working with the words, put them back into sentences.
7. Move to the other sentence level. At this stage *you* build the sentences (with the help of prompts). This is a turning point from the input to the output where you can use what you have learned so far.
8. Conclude your journey when you are able to produce your own speech in written and spoken forms that mirrors the input—the initial text of the lesson. That is your output. It shows the fruit of your learning in each lesson.

The lessons are organized in a way that they help gradually expand speech on the sentence level: from an imperative sentence made up of a verb (V) to a simple sentence with the subject + verb (S+V) and subject + verb + object (S+V+O) word order, furnished with the articles, adjectives, and adverbs; then connecting simple sentences into compound and complex sentences, and finally connecting them on the text level.

Studying one lesson may take many hours. It's recommended that you learn slowly, thoughtfully, with patience and faith.

The workbook ends with a celebration. You're invited to celebrate your knowledge of the English sounds, letters, and words as well as your skills of spoken and written English through various interesting tasks and activities.

Who is this course for?

This course is prepared for the audience with the intention of learning English seriously and intellectually. It's for those who would like to keep on studying English to as far as the advanced level. This workbook is not intended as a quick guide of tourist English.

The following symbols are used with the following meanings:

Symbols	Meanings
→	an arrow shows progression from … to …
=	an equal sign refers to a meaning
/i/	slashes are used for sounds
"a"	quotation marks are used for letters
'words'	words are enclosed in apostrophes
/wɜ-dz/	slashes contain phonetic pronunciation of words
/'/	a tick shows a word stress placed next to the stressed syllable

Before you get started, you need to know the meanings of the following linguistic terms:

Imperative sentence = _____

Simple sentence = _____

Affirmative sentence = _____

Negative sentence = _____

Word/words = _____

Letter/letters = _____

Sound/sounds = _____

Vowel/vowels = _____

Consonant/consonants = _____

Syllable/syllables = _____

Verb/verbs = _____

Pronoun/pronouns = _____

Noun/nouns = _____

Adjective/adjectives = _____

Adverb/adverbs = _____

(**Note**: some images used in this workbook are from pexels.com)

Lesson 1

Text: "**At the Computer**"

Imperative sentence: **Verb**…! ➔ Simple sentence: **I** + **verb**…

Words—letters—sounds:

Hell**o**—"o"—/oʊ/; c**o**py—"o"—/ɑ/; th**e**se—"e"—/i/; **th**ese—"th"—/ð/

---

1. Text

"At the Computer"

Listen to the text!

Read the text!

Hello! Follow these commands:
- Open your computer.
- Open an online translator.
- Highlight and copy the book introduction from the author website. (Or use your phone camera.)
- Paste the introduction for translation.
- Read the translation.
- Save the document.
- Close your computer.

Information: the letter "c" before the letters "o" "l" ➔ /k/: computer, copy, close…

Look up (translate) the following verbs from the text:

1. follow = _____
2. open = _____
3. highlight = _____
4. copy = _____
5. paste = _____
6. use = _____
7. save = _____
8. close = _____

2. Sentence

Imperative sentence (command, instruction): **V** (verb)! → **Follow**! Open! Highlight!

Highlight the <u>verbs</u> in these imperative sentences:

1. Open your computer.
2. Use your phone camera.
3. Highlight, copy, and paste!
4. Translate, read, and save!
5. Close your computer.

Read the following instructions about how to copy and paste:

1. Copy and paste!
2. Copy: Highlight the text. Press "command + C"!
3. Paste: Hold "command" and press "V"!

 **Write the names of these Mac computer commands**:

command + C = copy
command + V = _____
command + S = _____
command + O = _____
command + W = _____

3. Words

- **Verbs**: follow, open, highlight, copy, paste, use, save, close
- **Pronouns**: I – my, you – your; these
- **Articles**: the, a/an

Words	Letters	Sounds
Hell**o**, foll**ow**, **o**kay, cl**o**se, ph**o**ne	"o"	/oʊ/: back diphthong, long, tense
F**o**llow, c**o**py, **o**nline, st**o**p, sh**o**p	"o"	/ɑ/: low, open, tense vowel
P**a**ste, s**a**ve, pl**a**ce, s**a**le, m**a**ke	"a"	/eɪ/: front diphthong, long, tense
The, **th**ese, **th**en, **th**em, **th**ose	"th"	/ð/: interdental, voiced consonant
Th**e**se, m**e**, St**e**ve, P**e**te, sh**e**, h**e**	"e"	/i/: high, front, long, tense
End, pr**e**ss, p**e**n, g**e**t, n**e**t, t**e**ll, th**e**n	"e"	/ɛ/: mid-front, short, relaxed

Information: a diphthong = two vowels in one syllable

a syllable = one vowel with or without consonants

Antonyms: tense–relaxed; open–closed; front–back; high–low; short–long

Letters ➔ sounds:

Vowel letter "o" ➔ diphthong /oʊ/

Vowel letter "a" ➔ diphthong /eɪ/

Vowel letter "o" ➔ vowel sound /ɑ/

Vowel letter "e" ➔ vowel sound /i/

Vowel letter "e" ➔ vowel sound /ɛ/

Consonant letters "th" ➔ consonant sound /ð/

Open and closed syllables:

- open syllables: end in vowels or the silent letter "e" ➔ **long** vowel sounds or diphthongs (alphabet names): m**e**, h**e**, g**o**, n**o**; nam**e**, clos**e**, sav**e**, thes**e**
- closed syllables: closed by consonants ➔ **short** vowels: **e**nd, **i**t, **i**n, st**o**p

Open syllables:

The letter "o" ➔ /oʊ/: cl**o**se, s**o**, ph**o**ne; **but**: h**o**ld, t**o**ld (in closed syllables)

The letter "a" ➔ /eɪ/: p**a**ste, s**a**ve, m**a**ke, s**a**le, t**a**ke

The letter "e" ➔ /i/: th**e**se, St**e**ve, P**e**te, m**e**, h**e**, sh**e**

Closed syllables:

The letter "o" ➔ /ɑ/: **o**n, n**o**t, l**o**t, d**o**t; **but**: c**o**py, b**o**dy (in open syllables)

The letter "e" ➔ /ɛ/: **e**nd, p**e**n, th**e**n, pr**e**ss, g**e**t, n**e**t

Sounds → words:
- tense vowels /oʊ/, /ɑ/, /i/
- voiced consonant /ð/

Locate the vowel sounds /oʊ/, /ɑ/, /i/, /eɪ/, /ɛ/ in this American English Vowel Chart:

Tongue position	Front	Central	Back
High	/i/: long, closed, tense /ɪ/: short, relaxed		/u/: long, tense /ʊ/: short, relaxed
Mid	/ɛ/: short, relaxed /eɪ/: long, tense	/ʌ//ə/: short, relaxed /ɝ/: tense /ɚ/: short, relaxed	/oʊ/: long, tense
Low	/æ/: open, relaxed	/ɑ/: open, tense	/ɔ/: tense, open

Observe how the sounds /oʊ/, /ɑ/, /i/, /ð/ look:

1. Vowel (diphthong) **/oʊ/:**

/o/ + /ʊ/

→ the letter "o" in **open** syllables: **o**pen, cl**o**se /kloʊz/, he'll**o**, **o**'kay, foll**o**w; in **closed** syllables: h**o**ld /hoʊld/, t**o**ld

2. Vowel /ɑ/:

/ɑ/

→ the letter "o" in **closed** syllables: st**o**p, sh**o**p, n**o**t; in **open** syllables: c**o**py /'kɑpi/, b**o**dy, f**o**llow /'fɑloʊ/, **o**n'line

3. Vowel /i/ (long = the length of a smile)

/i/

➔ the letters "e" "y" in **open** syllables: th**e**se, m**e**, cop**y**

4. Consonant /ð/ (place the tip of the tongue between the teeth and say /zzzzz/)

/ð/

➔ the letters "th": **th**e, **th**ese, **th**ose, **th**en, **th**em

Read the following words with the sounds /oʊ/, /ɑ/, /i/, /ð/:

Open, close, so, no, note, cope, go, those, hold
Copy, doc, d**o**cument, dot, not, top, stop, shop, lot, body, on, online
Me, she, he, be, Pete, Steve, these
These, those, them, then

Read the following words with the open and closed syllables:

Cope – cop; so – sod; no – not; go – got; note – not

Read the following words with the sounds /eɪ/, /aɪ/, /ɛ/, /ju/:

Ok**ay**, say, stay, paste, save, make, sale, place, take
I, my, write /raɪt/, file, find, hi**gh**, li**gh**t, highlight /ˈhaɪlaɪt/ ("gh"– silent letters)
End, get, pen, pet, bet, met, leg, check, net
You, computer, **u**se, document

Letters ➔ words:
- vowels: A, E, I, O, U
- consonants: C, D, L, M, N, P, S, V

Write the letters for these sounds. **Example**: /si/ – C

Vowels: /oʊ/ – _____; /eɪ/ – _____; /ju/ – _____; /aɪ/ – _____; /i/ – _____
Consonants: /pi/ – ___; /ɛs/ – ___; /ɛm/ – ___; /vi/ – ___; /ɛn/ ___ /di/ – ___; /ɛl/ – ___

Write the missing letters in these verbs:

F__llow; __pen; c__py; p__ste; s__ve; cl__se

Complete these words:

Cl_____; s_____; th_____; o_____; hi_____; u_____

Write antonyms for these words:

Open–_____; offline–_____; hold–_____; stop–_____

4. Sentence

Imperative sentence: **V** (verb) ➜ Simple sentence: **S** (subject) + **V** (verb).
    S: I/You + **V**: copy, paste, save, highlight = I copy.

    Highlight! ➜ **You** highlight.
    Copy! ➜ **I** copy.
    Paste! ➜ **You** paste.
    Save! ➜ **I** save.

Form simple sentences. **Example**: Save and close! ➜ I save and close.

1. Highlight. ➜ _____
2. Copy. ➜ _____
3. Paste and close! ➜ _____

Complete the sentences. Use these verbs "open, close, copy, paste, go, stop":

I _____, you _____.
I _____, you _____.
I _____, you _____.

Read these sentences. Follow the intonation: rising ↗ or falling ↘.

↘Open! I ↘open. I ↗open, you ↘close. ↘Copy! You ↗copy and ↘paste.
You ↘follow me. ↘Highlight! You ↗highlight, then I ↗copy and ↘paste.

Read these sentences with the rising and/or falling intonation:

Follow me! I follow you. You copy and paste. I save and close.

Rewrite these sentences in logical order:

1. I highlight the text.
2. I close my computer.
3. I open my computer.
4. I paste the text.
5. I follow the instructions.
6. I save the document.
7. I copy the text.

1. _____
2. _____
3. _____
4. _____
5. _____
6. _____
7. _____

5. Text

Write about how you work on the computer!

I open…

Speak! Use the following order:

1. ____ open _____
2. ____ follow _____
3. ____ highlight _____
4. ____ copy _____
5. ____ close _____

Homework:
1. Read about the difference between letters and sounds, vowels and consonants.
2. Find the "Sounds American" channel online. Watch the videos about the sounds: /ð/–/ɑ/–/ɛ/–/i/ and diphthongs /oʊ/–/eɪ/–/aɪ/.

Lesson 2

Text: **In Class**
Simple affirmative sentence: **I/You/We/They** + **verb** (base form) + noun.
Verbs: the Present Simple tense
Nouns: singular ➔ plural
Words—letters—sounds:
Teach—"t"—/t/; **w**elcome—"w"—/w/; **r**ead—"r"—/r/
Class—"a"—/æ/; **E**nglish—"e" "i"—/ɪ/; st**o**ry—"o"—/ɔ/; l**oo**k—"oo"—/ʊ/

---

1. Text

"In Class"

Look at the teacher!   **Listen to and/or read her story**.

Hello, all!
I teach English. I plan lessons.
In class, I welcome my students. I tell them good stories. They listen and talk. Then we open books and read. We also write. I like my students. I like English and I like to teach English.

Look up these words from the text. Write down their translations:

1. all = _____
2. teach = _____
3. welcome = _____
4. tell = _____
5. story/stories = _____
6. talk = _____
7. book/books = _____
8. also = _____
9. like = _____

Classify these words as <u>pronouns</u>, <u>verbs</u>, and <u>nouns</u>. Write them in the table:

Welcome, we, student, they, them, book, I, tell, speak, teach, write, you, story, listen, lesson, class, my, English

Pronouns	Verbs	Nouns

2. Sentence

Present time → the Present Simple tense → common actions, events, facts

Affirmative sentence: **S** (Pronoun/noun) + **V** (base form) + **O** (pronoun/noun).
Pronouns (I/You/We/They) + **verbs** (plan/like/read/tell) + **nouns** (books/stories)
→ I teach English. You like English. We read books. They tell stories.

Highlight the <u>pronouns</u> and <u>nouns</u> in these statements:

1. I teach English.
2. I plan lessons.
3. We welcome the teacher.
4. You read books.
5. They write stories.
6. We listen to the teacher.
7. The students like English.

3. Words

- **Personal pronouns (Subjects):** I — you — we — they
- **Personal pronouns (Objects):** me — you — us — them
- **Possessive pronouns** (before nouns): my — your — our — their

Compare personal and possessive pronouns:

Singular: I /aɪ/, me /mi/ → my /maɪ/; you /ju/, you → your /jɔr/

Plural: We, us /ʌs/→our /ɑr//aʊr/; you, you→your; they /ðeɪ/, them→their /ðɜr/

Fit the possessive pronouns "your, my, our, their" **into these sentences**:

I welcome _____ students. You read _____ book. We tell _____ stories. You read _____ books. They write _____ stories.

Words	Letters	Sounds
Class, plan, task, stand	"a"	/æ/: low, front, open, relaxed
Book, look, put, pull, push	"oo" "ou" "u" "o"	/ʊ/: high, back, short, relaxed
Listen, English, in, big, fit	"e" "i"	/ɪ/: high, front, short, relaxed
Story, sorry, all, call, law	"o" "a" "aw" "au"	/ɔ/: low, back, open, tense
Teach, tell, time, table	"t"	/t/: alveolar, aspirated consonant
Welcome, we, well, wall	"w"	/w/ (unusual consonant sound)
Read, write, story, sorry	"r" "wr" (silent "w")	/r/ (unusual consonant sound)

Letters ➔ sounds:
Vowel letter: "a" ➔ vowel sound /æ/
Vowel letters: "oo" "u" "o" ➔ vowel sound /ʊ/
Vowel letters: "i" "e" ➔ vowel sound /ɪ/
Vowel letters: "o" "a" "aw" "au" ➔ vowel sound /ɔ/
Consonants: "t" ➔ /t/; "w" ➔ /w/; "r" "wr" ➔ /r/

Syllables with two vowel letters together:
- the first vowel: ➔ pronounced (as in the alphabet), the second: ➔ silent: teach, speak, read, meal, people, main, coat, see, seen, bee, deed, meal, please...
- diphthongs: /ɔɪ/: boil, boy; /aʊ/: out, house; /aɪ/: eye, guy...

Please highlight the vowel letters that sound in these words:

Boat, coat, goat, pain, mail, gain, team, feat, clean, deed, feet, meet, people

Please write the diphthongs /ɔɪ, aʊ, aɪ/ next to the words that have them:

About _____, boy _____, coin _____, guy _____, house _____, file _____, loud_____

Sounds → words:

- consonants /t/, /w/, /r/
- short, relaxed vowels /æ/, /ʊ/, /ɪ/; tense vowel /ɔ/ (Locate these vowel sounds in the "American English Vowel Chart" on page 11.)

1. Consonant /t/ (alveolar sound) → the letter "t": **t**each, **t**ell, **t**ea, **t**able, **t**ime, **t**est

How to pronounce **alveolar** consonants: /t/, /d/, /s/, /z/, /n/, /l/?
Touch the alveolar ridge (above the upper teeth) with the tip of your tongue.

Touch the alveolar ridge with the tip of your tongue and pronounce the sounds:
/t/, /d/, /s/, /z/, /n/, /l/

Read the following words with the alveolar consonants:

Table, **t**est, **d**ee**d**, **s**mile, **z**one, **z**est, **n**o, **n**ose, **l**et, **l**eave

2. Consonant /w/ → the letter "w" ('double-u): **w**elcome, **w**e, **w**ait, **w**in, **w**ell, **w**ill

How to pronounce the /**w**/ sound?
Form your lips into a small circle and imagine whistling. Quickly pull your lips in a smile and say: **W**e **w**in.

Look up these words in the dictionary. Write down their translations:

1. win	1. _____
2. wait	2. _____
3. week	3. _____
4. want	4. _____
5. walk	5. _____
6. weak	6. _____
7. wish	7. _____

Read the following words with the sound /w/:

We, well, welcome /ˈwɛlkəm/, weak, week, wait, win, wish

Begin these sentences with the pronoun We:

____ welcome you. ____ wait. ____ will wait. ____ will win.

3. Consonant /r/ ➔ the letter "r": read, red, race, rate, rain, rail, road, ˈrailroad

---

How to pronounce the **/r/** sound?

Raise the tip of the tongue and curl it **a little** back behind the upper tooth ridge and pronounce /rrrrr/ without touching the top of your mouth.

Important: Never touch the teeth or the tooth ridge with the tip of the tongue!

Read the following words with the sound /r/:

Read – write /raɪt/ – rain – race – ray – raise – red – road

Reˈmember the correct stress in these words:

Reˈread, reˈwrite, reˈopen, reˈtype, reˈpeat

Information: the prefix 're-' ➔ /ri/ or /rə/ = again.

Look up these words in the dictionary. Write the missing phonetic pronunciation:

1. Repeat /rəˈpit/	1. _____
2. React /riˈækt/	2. _____
3. Reflect /_____/	3. _____
4. Respect /_____/	4. _____
5. Remember /_____/	5. _____
6. Request /rəˈkwest/	6. _____
7. Review /rəˈvju/	7. _____

4. Vowel /æ/ (low, front, open, relaxed)

/æ/

→ in **closed** syllables: cl**a**ss, pl**a**n, st**a**nd, **a**dd, **a**pple, b**a**g, c**a**p, c**a**t, fl**a**g, m**a**p, t**a**sk...
but: h**a**ve (in open syllable)

Remember: the letter "c" → /k/ before the letters "o" "a" "u" "l" "r" "t": copy, cat, cute, class, crop, fact; but the letter "c" → /s/ before the letters "e" "i" "y": cent, pencil, cycle…

Write these words "apple, bag, cap, cat, flag, map" **under the correct pictures**:

_____ _____ _____ _____ _____ _____

5. Vowel /ɔ/ (low, *back*, open, tense)

/ɔ/

→ in **closed** syllables: **a**ll, **a**lso, b**a**ll, c**a**ll, l**a**wn, f**a**ult, d**o**g, b**o**ss, talk /tɔk/, walk /wɔk/ (silent "l"); in **open** syllables: st**o**ry, s**o**rry, dr**a**w, l**a**w, str**a**w, r**a**w, s**a**w, **au**to, **au**dio

Write these words "ball, dog, clock, coffee, door" **under the correct pictures**:

_____ _____ _____ _____ _____

Read these words with the sound /ɔ/:

All, 'also, 'al,ways, ,al'ready, auto, 'audiobook, ball, call, small, saw, law, draw, fault, want, 'coffee, clock, chalk (silent "l"), walk, talk

Observe and compare how the sounds /ɑ/ – /ɔ/ – /æ/ look. Read the words in the table row by row:

/ɑ/	/ɔ/	/æ/
Copy	Auto	Ask
Body	Long	Back
Box	Small	Bag
Job	Fall	Bad
Not	Tall	Pass
Rock	Dog	Pat
Pot	Office	Stand

6. Vowel /ʊ/ (high, back, short, relaxed)

/ʊ/

➔ in **closed** syllables: b**oo**k, full, pull, put, push; in **open** syllables: w**o**man, sugar, cushion, pudding

Remember the following words with the sound /ʊ/:

"**oo**": book, good, poor, cook, foot, hook, look, shook, stood, took, wood, wool
"**ou**": could /kʊd, would /wʊd/, should /ʃʊd/
"**o**": wolf, woman /'wʊmən/
"**u**": bull, bullet, bush, cushion, full, pudding, pull, push, put, sugar

Use the word "good" with all these words:

_____ book; _____ cook; _____ woman; _____ cushion; _____ pudding

Observe how the sounds /u/ and /ʊ/ look. Compare them:

/u/   /ʊ/

- Sound /u/ (high, back, *long*, *tense*)
- Sound /ʊ/ (high, back, *short*, *relaxed*)

Read these words with the sounds /u/ and /ʊ/:

/u/: do, too, food, zoom, pool, move, mood, due, new, news
/ʊ/: put, book, good, goods, could, would, should, woman

Read these minimal pairs with the sounds /u/ and /ʊ/: pool – pull; fool – full.

7. Vowel /ɪ/ (high, front, short, relaxed)

➔ in **closed** syllables: English, listen /ˈlɪsn/, it, is, chip, big, fill, fit, sit, his... **but:** live /lɪv/, give /gɪv/ (in open syllables)

Observe how the sounds /ɪ/ and /i/ look. Compare them:

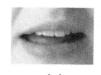

/ɪ/   /i/

- Sound /ɪ/ (high, front, *short*, *relaxed*)
- Sound /i/ (high, front, *long*, *tense*)

Read these minimal pairs with the sounds /ɪ/ and /i/:

Fill – feel; mill – meal; bin – bean; chip – cheap; it – eat; is – ease; sit – seat
Lip – leap; did – deed; fit – feet; hit – heat, dip – deep; grin – green, this – these

Important information: Words never end in vowels: /ɪ/, /ɛ/, /æ/, /ʊ/.

Letters → words:
- vowels
- spelling (naming the letters that form a word)

Write the phonetic pronunciation of the vowel letters only. Example: Y /waɪ/

A /___/ C ___ D ___ E ___ F ___ I ___ N ___ O ___ P ___ R ___ S ___ T ___
U ___ V ___ W ___ X ___ Z

Spell these words: English, listen, read, write, speak, tell, story, book, like, talk

Nouns
Singular → Plural:
1. Add the suffix "-s/-es" to singular nouns!
2. Pronounce the suffix "-s/es" as:
   - /z/ after the vowels and voiced consonants: stories, words
   - /ɪz/ after the letters: "ce" "ss" "sh" "ch" "x" "z": boxes, sentences
   - /s/ after the voiceless/unvoiced consonants: books, students

---

Voiced consonants (sound, vibration of vocal cords): /b, d, g, dʒ, v, ð, z, ʒ, m, n, ŋ, l/
Voiceless consonants (no sound, no vibration of vocal cords, air): /p, t, k, tʃ, f, θ, s, ʃ/

Observe singular nouns → plural nouns:
command → commands /dz/
book → books /ks/
story → stories /z/ ("y" → "ie")
word → words /z/
sentence → sentences /ɪz/
box → boxes /ɪz/
But: woman → women; man → men; foot → feet…

Write the plurals of the following nouns:

Instruction – _____; lesson – _____; sign /saɪn/ – _____
Command – _____; word – _____; sound – _____
Student – _____; consonant – _____
Book – _____; text – _____; clock – _____
Class – _____; box – _____; sentence – _____
Computer – _____; teacher – _____
Story – _____; company – _____
Woman – _____; man – _____; foot – _____

4. Sentence

Look at these signs. Read the verbs on the signs. Finish the sentences below:

I see the sign "_____." I _____. I _____, then I _____.

Read these sentences with the rising ↗ and falling ↘ intonation:

I see the sign Road ↗Closed, I ↘slow. I ↗stop, then I ↘go.

Highlight the sentences that describe English lessons only:

We welcome our English teacher. We stop at the Stop sign. We listen to the stories in English. We see the closed road. We open our English books. We slow and stop. Then we go. We read English texts. We write and speak in English. We all like English. We like to speak in English.

Speak about what you like to do at your English lessons. For example: I like **to** watch videos in English. ('**to**' before the verb = the infinitive)

1. I like my English lessons.
2. I like to _____
3. I also like to _____

Finish the following sentences with these words: English teacher, audiobooks and podcasts, English, videos and movies, books, stories, English lessons.

1. We welcome our _____
2. We listen **to** _____
3. You speak _____
4. They watch good _____
5. We read English _____
6. Students tell good _____
7. We like our _____

5. Text

Fill in the blanks in the following story:

I like ____ _____ lessons. In _____ English classes, we _____, read, write, and _____. We also tell good _____. We like _____.

Write a story about your English lessons.

I like English. I take English lessons. In class, we…

Speak about your English lessons. Begin:

1. I _____
2. We _____
3. The students _____
4. They _____
5. You _____

Homework:
1. Watch the "Sounds American" videos that practice the sounds: /æ/ /ɔ/ /ʊ/ (/ʊ/-/u/) /ɪ/ (/ɪ/-/i/) /t/ /r/ /w/
2. Further read about the formation of plural nouns (in your first language).

Lesson 3

Text: **At Work**

Negatives and questions with the verb '**do**' (Present Simple tense):
- I/You/We/They **don't** (**do not**) + (adverb) + verb…
- **Do** I/you/we/they + (adverb) + verb…?
- What **do** I/you/we/they + (adverb) + verb…?

Adverbs of frequency: always, usually, often, sometimes, rarely, never

Words—letters—sounds:

Work—"or"—/wɝ/; f**ir**st, p**er**son, s**ure**—"ir" "er" "ur"—/ɝ/; driv**er,** per'cent—"er"—/ɚ/
H**ere**—"er"—/ɪr/; c**ar**—"ar"—/ɑr/; sh**ort**—"or"—/ɔr/; c**arr**y—"ar"—/ɛr/

---

1. Text

"At Work"

(Photo by W. Fortunato from Pexels)

> Two guys meet at the shipping company for the first time.
>
> Person A: Hi! Do you work here?
> Person B: Yes, I do.
>   A: What do you do?
>   B: I work as a driver.
>   A: Do you drive a car?
>   B: No, I do not. I drive a truck.
>   A: You do! Do you rent a truck?
>   B: No, I don't. I don't rent a truck. I own the truck.
>   A: Do you drive short or long distances?
>   B: I specialize in long distance driving services.
>   A: What do you generally do at work?
>   B: I generally carry and deliver commercial products.
>   A: Thank you. Nice to meet you.
>   B: Sure. Nice to meet you too.

Highlight these phrases in the dialog. Look them up and write their translations:

1. for the first time = _____
2. work here = _____
3. work as a driver = _____
4. drive a car/truck = _____
5. at work = _____
6. deliver commercial products = _____
7. nice to meet you = _____

Write the words "deliver, a truck, carry, a driver, a car" **under the correct pictures**:

_____ _____ _____ _____ _____

Match the opposites in this table. Draw lines to connect them:

1. Service	A. Rent
2. Work	B. Car
3. Own	C. Product
4. Drive	D. Long distance
5. First	E. Last
6. Truck	F. Walk
7. Short distance	G. Rest

Write the plurals of these nouns:

Company – _____
Service – _____
Distance – _____
Product – _____
Car – _____
Driver – _____
Truck – _____

2. Sentence

Types of sentences:

Affirmative sentence: I/You/They/We + verb... ➜ We work here.
Negative sentence: I/You/They/We **don't (do not)** + verb... ➜ They **don't** work here.
Yes/No question: **Do** you/they/we/I + verb...? ➜ **Do** you work here?
Wh-question: What **do** you/they/we/I + verb...? ➜ What **do** you do here?

Compare the affirmative and negative sentences:

1. I work here. You don't work here.
2. I drive a truck. I do not drive a car.
3. I own the truck. I don't rent a truck.
4. I drive long distances. I do not drive short distances.

How to form **negative** sentences?

Affirmative sentence: I/You/They/We + verb... ➜ Negative sentence: I/You/They/We **do not (don't)** + verb...

1. I drive a ⤵truck. ➜ I ⤵**don't** drive a car.
2. You work at ⤵home. ➜ You **do** ⤵**not** work at the office.

Information: do not ➜ don't = contraction; ['] = apostrophe

Write the matching answers to these questions from the dialog on page 26:

For example: Question: Do you work here? Answer: Yes, I do.

1. Do you work here? _____
2. Do you drive a car? _____
3. Do you rent a truck? _____
4. Do you drive short or long distances? _____
5. Do you specialize in long distance driving services? _____
6. What do you do? _____
7. What do you generally do at work? _____

Write the matching yes/no questions from the dialog to these answers:

1. _____? Yes, I do.
2. _____? No, I do not. I drive a truck.
3. _____? No, I don't. I own the truck.

Write the matching wh-questions from the dialog to these answers:

- _____? I work as a driver.
- _____? I carry and deliver commercial products.

How to ask and answer **questions**?

Statement (simple sentence): I/You/They/We + verb…
➔ Yes/No question: **Do** you/they/we/I + verb…?
                     Yes, I/you do./No, they/we don't.
➔ Wh-question: What /wʌt/ **do** you/they/we/I + verb...?
                     I/You/They/We + verb...

1. **Do** you work ↗here? ↘Yes, I ↘do./↗No, I do ↘not (↘don't).
2. **Do** you drive ↗short **or*** ↘long distances? I drive ↘long distances.
3. What **do*** you ↘do**? I work as a ↘truck driver.

*this or that question (alternative question)
**do = helping verb (auxiliary verb)
***do = main verb (meaningful verb)

Answer these questions based on your personal situation:

1. What do you do? _____
2. Where do you work? _____
3. What company do you work at? _____
4. What do you generally do at work? _____
5. Do you work from home? _____
6. Do you work at home or at the office? _____
7. Do you drive to your work? _____
8. What car do you drive? _____
9. Do you own or do you rent your car? _____

3. Words

Words	Letters	Sounds
Work, **wor**d, **wor**ld, **wor**st	"wor"	/wɝ/: /w/+/ɝ/
F**ir**st, th**ir**d, p**er**son, s**er**vice, s**ur**e, b**ur**n	"ir" "er" "ur"	/ɝ/: **one** tense sound, in stressed syllables
Driv**er**, deliv**er**, p**er**cent, col**or**	"er" "or"	/ɚ/: **one** relaxed sound, in unstressed syllables
H**er**e, y**ear**, cl**ear**, p**er**iod	"er" "ear"	/ɪr/: diphthong /ɪ/+/r/
C**ar**, f**ar**m, f**ar**, st**ar**, ch**ar**t	"ar"	/ɑr/: diphthong /ɑ/+/r/
Sh**or**t, **or**, st**or**e, f**or**m, w**ar**m	"or" "ar"	/ɔr/: diphthong /ɔ/+/r/
C**ar**ry, wh**er**e, ch**air**, p**ear**, th**eir**	"ar" "er" "air" "ear" "eir"	/ɛr/: diphthong /ɛ/+/r/

Classify the following words as <u>one syllable</u> **or** <u>two syllable</u> **words. Write them in the table below. Put a word stress /ˈ/ on or next to the stressed syllables:**

Drive, driver, driving, short, long, service, carry, carrier, deliver, sure, person, truck, trucking, work, worker, serve, service, read, reader, own, owner, distance

One syllable words	Two syllable words
Drive...	ˈDriver...

Letters → sounds:
Letters "wor" → sounds /wɝ/
Letters "ir" "ur" "er" → sound /ɝ/
Letters "er" "or" → sound /ɚ/
Letters "er" "ear" → diphthong /ɪr/

Letters "ar" ➔ diphthong /ɑr/
Letters "or" "ar" ➔ diphthong /ɔr/
Letters "air" "ear" "eir" "ar" "er" ➔ diphthong /ɛr/

Group these words with the letter "r" according to the types of syllables:

Rent, red, read, write, really, rain, rob, rude, rope, rice, room, race, road, ride, rod

1. **Open syllables**: write…
2. **Closed syllables**: red…
3. **Two vowel letter syllables**: read…

---

4. **R-controlled syllables**:
   In r-controlled syllables, vowels + the letter "r" = **r-controlled** (r-colored) vowels.
   Vowels followed by the letter "r" **merge** with /r/ and become:
   - one sound: /ɝ/ ➔ in stressed syllables "ir" "er" "ur": g**ir**l, c**ir**cle, ʹp**er**son, ʹs**er**vice, s**u**re, b**ur**n, w**or**ld, w**o**rry /ʹwɝri/
   - one sound: /ɚ/ ➔ in unstressed syllables "er" "ur" "or": driv**er**, teach**er**, dinn**er**, sur'prise, col**or**, commentat**or**
   - diphthongs: /ɪr/, /ɑr/, /ɔr/, /ɛr/ ➔ in stressed syllables "er" "ar" "or" "air": h**ere**, y**ear**, c**ar**, ch**ar**t, sh**or**t, p**or**t, **or**, st**ore**, undersc**ore**, th**ere**

Circle the words with the sounds /ɝ/ and /wɝ/ only:

Order, first, service, farm, firm, burn, cart, word, worst, skirt, start, stir, store, girl

Circle the words with the sound /ɚ/ only:

Color, turn, third, teacher, burn, for, fur, worker, curb, clerk, surprise, driver, dinner

Circle the words with the diphthongs /ɪr/, /ɑr/, /ɔr/, /ɛr/ only:

Art, are, form, floor, chart, or, more, here, bird, star, their, person, far, carry, marry

Sounds ➔ words:
- aspirated (plosive) consonants: (voiced) **/g/, /b/, /d/**; (voiceless) **/k/, /p/, /t/**
- consonant clusters: **/tr/, /dr/, /br/, /gr/, /pr/, /kr/**
- r-controlled vowels: **/ɝ/, /ɚ/** (Locate the vowel sounds /ɝ/ and /ɚ/ in the "American English Vowel Chart" on page 11.)
- diphthongs: **/ɪr/, /ɑr/, /ɔr/, /ɛr/**

1. Aspirated consonants: /g/, /b/, /d/, /k/, /p/, /t/ ➔ the letters "g" "b" "d" "k/c" "p" "t": **g**o, **b**ig, **d**o, **k**it/**c**all, **p**lace, **t**each

---

How to pronounce **aspirated** consonant sounds?

Aspiration = a small puff of air coming from the mouth with an exhalation of breath (like the sound /h/).

Consonants /g/, /b/, /d/, /k/, /p/, /t/ ➔ aspirated only:
- at the beginning of words: **p**art, **b**ig, **d**oll, **t**eacher, **c**all, **g**irl
- in stressed syllables: i**d**ea, sur**p**rise...

No aspiration:
  ➔ when the words begin with the letter "s": student, store, stop
  ➔ at the end of words: bag, keep, meet (final stop consonants)

Pronounce these consonants with a small puff of air (aspiration):
  /b/, /d/, /g/, /t/, /k/, /p/

Read the following words, aspirating the first consonants only:

  Pen, dad, cat, post, bag, pick, big, take, boy, top, dot, cook, get, talk, kid, keep

2. Consonant clusters: /tr/*, /dr/*, /br/, /gr/, /pr/, /kr/
(*/tr/ ➔ /tʃr/ and /dr/ ➔ /dʒr/)

Read the words with the letter "r" in combination with the aspirated consonants:

  /tr/ —"tr"—**tr**uck: tree, trunk, transit, train, trash, trick, trip, true, tray, treat
  /dr/ —"dr"—**dr**ive: drink, draw, dream, dress, dry, drop, drag, drain
  /br/—"br"—**br**ing: break, bread, bridge, brief, breakfast, brown, breeze, branch
  /gr/—"gr"—**gr**eat: green, grass, grapes, grab, grow, grade, grain, grand
  /pr/— "pr"—**pr**ide: problem, press, price, pray, prime, print, prince, prop, praise
  /kr/— "cr"—**cr**eam: crib, crawl, creep, crown, crab, critical, cross

3. Vowel /ɝ/ ➔ the letters "er" "ir" "ur": p**er**son, g**ir**l, b**ur**n, s**er**vice, sh**ir**t, s**ur**e
                    the letters "or" after the letter "w": w**or**k, w**or**d, w**or**ld, w**or**ry, w**or**st
4. Vowel /ɚ/ ➔ the letters "er""ur" "or": driv**er**, teach**er**, s**ur**'prise, col**or**, dinn**er**

How to pronounce the **sounds /ɝ/ and /ɚ/?**

Curl the tip of your tongue **a little** bit back without touching your upper front teeth, tense your tongue as in /r/. Round and slightly protrude your lips. Make the sound /ɛ/ with the overtone of /r/ = /ɝ/ ➔ in stressed syllables.

The sound /ɚ/: similar to /ɝ/ but relaxed and quick ➔ in unstressed syllables.

Read the following words with the sounds /wɝ/, /ɝ/, and /ɚ/:

/wɝ/—**wor**k: word, world, worm, worst, worry
/ɝ/—**fir**st: girl, dirt, bird, shirt, skirt, firm, stir
/ɝ/—**sur**e: burn, fur, curb, turtle, further, nurse, hurt, turn
/ɝ/—cl**er**k, person, service, her, observe, learn /lɝn/
/ɚ/—driv**er**: deliver, father, teacher, finger, super, dinner, helper
/ɚ/—col**or**: accelerator, commentator, accumulator

5. Diphthongs /ɪr/, /ɑr/, /ɔr/, /ɛr/ ➔ the letters "er" "ar" "or" "eir": h**ere**, c**ar**, **or**, th**eir**

Read the following words with the diphthongs /ɪr/, /ɑr/, /ɔr/, /ɛr/:

/ɪr/—"er" "ear"—h**ere**: zero, hero, dear, clear, ear, hear, near, fear
/ɑr/—"ar"—c**ar**: farm, farmer, far, star, chart, hard, art, are, start
/ɔr/—"or"—sh**ort**: or, for, store, score, corn, cord, form, door, sport
/ɛr/—"ar" "er" "air"—c**ar**ry: marry, area, their, there, air, hair, chair

Letters ➔ words:
- consonants
- alphabetical order

Write the phonetic pronunciation of the consonants only. For example: Z /zi/

A ___ B ___ C ___ D ___ E ___ F ___ G ___ H ___ I ___ J ___ K ___ L ___ M ___
N ___ O ___ P ___ Q ___ R ___ S ___ T ___ U ___ V ___ W ___ X ___ Y ___ Z ___

Put the following words in alphabetical order and write them on the lines below:

Hot, call, apple, food, tea, good, say, miss, desk, pen, week, red, eat, it, look, okay, bag, use, yes, zeal, job, van, lid

_____

_____

Word formation:

- the suffixes '-er' '-or' '-ar' ➔ often form the names of occupations and professions

Highlight the words that name a person only:

Driver, teacher, deliver, computer, super, weather, dinner, supper, farmer, worker, owner, reader, writer, helper, never, waiter, letter

Form and write the names of occupations with the help of the suffix '-er' (-r):

Drive: _____; teach: _____; wait: _____

Listen: _____; read: _____; write: _____; speak: _____

Tell: _____; work: _____; farm: _____

Own: _____; rent: _____; deliver: _____

4. Sentence

Choose one of the words in parentheses and complete these sentences:

I _____ English. (teach/learn)
I _____ a car. (rent/own)
I drive _____. (a car/a truck)
We learn _____. (English/French)
They _____ books. (read/write)
You work as _____. (a teacher/a driver)

Write that I/You/We/They **don't do that**. Write what I/You/We/They **do instead**:

1. I go to the office. You _____. You _____ at home.
2. You drive a van. I _____. I _____ a truck.
3. You work at the office. I _____. I _____ from home.
4. We work here. You _____. You _____ there.
5. They specialize in services. They _____. They _____ in products.

Circle only the helping verb 'do' in these sentences:

1. I do my homework.
2. I don't do my homework.
3. Do you do your homework?
4. What do you do after your English classes?

Identify the types of sentences. Use these signs:

> - [!] → imperatives
> - [+] → affirmatives
> - [-] → negatives
> - [yes/no?] → yes/no questions
> - [or?] → alternative/choice questions
> - [wh?] → wh-questions

1. What language do you learn? _____
2. Do you learn English or do you learn French? _____
3. I learn English. _____
4. Learn English! _____
5. Do you teach English? _____
6. I don't teach English. _____

Read these sentences with the rising and/or falling intonation:

1. Do you drive a ↗car? ↘Yes, I ↘do. ↘No, I ↘don't.
2. Do you drive a ↗car or a ↘truck?
3. What do you ↘drive?
4. I drive a ↘truck. I do ↘not drive a van.
5. I don't work at the ↘office.

Disagree with the following statements. Write the correct information:

Waiters teach students. _____. Teachers teach students.
Teachers deliver goods. _____. _____
Farmers write books. _____. _____
Drivers serve food. _____. _____
Writers drive trucks. _____. _____
Tellers tell stories. _____. Storytellers _____

Read through and complete this dialog with the missing questions:

B: Hi. _____?
A: No, I don't.
B: _____?
A: I work as a computer person at an advertising agency.
B: _____?
A: No, I work from home.
B: Nice! So you don't work at the office! _____?
A: Not really. I don't normally like to work at home. I generally want to work in the office. Only sometimes I prefer to work from home.
B: Nice to meet you.
A: Nice to meet you too!

Note these words and phrases:

1. advertise = market, promote
2. advertising agency
3. prefer /prəˈfɚ/ = like

Observe the sentences with the verbs "like, prefer, want" **in the dialog above. Finish these sentences**:

- I don't normally like to _____
- I generally want to _____
- Only sometimes I prefer to _____

Adverbs of frequency (how often):
      always /ˈɔl,weɪz/ = all the time
      usually = generally, normally, regularly
      often = most of the time
      'some,times = from time to time
      rarely /ˈrɛrli/ = not often
      never = at no time

Put the adverbs of frequency on the relative scale:

Most frequent_____Least frequent

Speak about how often you like/prefer/want to do something. Answer these questions:

1. What do you **often** like to do?
2. What do you **never** like to do?
3. What do you **always** prefer to do?
4. What do you **sometimes** want to do?
5. What do you **rarely** want to do?
6. What do you **usually** prefer to do?

Rewrite these sentences including the adverbs of frequency in parentheses:

1. I study English after the lessons. (always) _____
2. We walk to work. (rarely) _____
3. They read and write. (sometimes) _____
4. I don't like to wait. (usually) _____
5. You work at home. (often) _____
6. They visit us. (never) _____

Connect these words into sentences following the correct word order:

- always, I, books, read _____
- meet, the guys, work, sometimes, at _____
- stories, often, tell, good, people _____
- we, speak, usually, and, in, listen, class _____
- parents, rarely, my, me, visit _____
- never, coffee, drink, they _____

Complete these sentences based on your personal situation:

- We always _____
- We do not always _____
- I usually _____
- I don't usually _____
- My friends don't often _____
- They often _____
- They sometimes _____
- I rarely _____
- I never _____

5. Text

Pretend that you work as a truck driver. Talk about your work. Follow these pictures:

Write a story about your work. Use these unfinished sentences:

I work at a _____

I work as a _____

I like/don't like my _____

I always _____

I often _____

I sometimes prefer to _____

I want to work at/for a/an _____ company.

Tell the story about your work. Use these questions as a plan for your story:

1. What do you do for a living?
2. What company do you work at/for?
3. What do you usually do at work?
4. What do you rarely do at work?
5. What do you never do at work?

Describe your day at work. Let the adverbs of frequency help you:

Always/never: _____

Often/usually: _____

Sometimes/rarely: _____

Thank you!

Homework:

1. Watch the "Sounds American" videos that practice the r-controlled (r-colored) vowels /wɝ/, /ɝ/, /ɚ/; diphthongs: /ɪr/, /ɑr/, /ɔr/, /ɛr/; consonant clusters: /tr/, /dr/.
2. Further read about how to form negatives and different types of questions.

Lesson 4

Text: **At Home**
Affirmatives, negatives, and questions with the verb '**does**' (Present Simple tense):
- She/He/It + verb(-**s/es**)…
- She/He/It **doesn't** (**does not**) + verb…
- **Does** she/he/it + verb…?
- What **does** she/he/it + verb…?

Numbers: cardinal → ordinal
Articles: the; a/an
Words—letters—sounds:
Home—"h"—/h/; **sh**e—"sh"— /ʃ/; d**o**es—"o"—/ʌ/; c**o**mputer—"o"—/ə/; **th**ree —"th"—/θ/

---

1. Text

"At Home"

Hello, friends! What do you like to do at home?
I like to spend time with my family. Well, I also like to watch TV.
In the picture, you see my family: my wife, my two sons, and me.
We celebrate our birthdays. We always celebrate our birthdays.
I work as a computer person at an advertising agency. My wife
doesn't work. She stays at home and watches the kids. She likes to cook and read.
My older son goes to school. He likes to play video games. My younger son prefers
to learn letters and numbers. Now you know my family.

Highlight the <u>sentences</u> with these words and phrases in the story above. Look them up and write their translations:

1. spend time = _____
2. in the picture = _____
3. wife (husband) = _____
4. son/sons = _____
5. celebrate = _____
6. stay at home = _____
7. watch TV/watch the kids = _____
8. know /noʊ/ ("k" – silent) = _____

Do you remember these words? Write the meanings (translations) of these words from the previous lessons. Don't look them up!

1.	Advertise	1.	_____
2.	Change	2.	_____
3.	Follow	3.	_____
4.	Prefer	4.	_____
5.	Remember	5.	_____
6.	Sometimes	6.	_____
7.	Rarely	7.	_____

2. Sentence

Present time ➜ the Present Simple tense ➜ the third person singular

Affirmative sentence: She/He/It + verb(**s/es**)… ➜ He cook**s**. She watch**es** TV.
Negative sentence: She/He/It **doesn't (does not)** + verb… ➜ She **doesn't** cook.
Yes/No question: **Does** she/he/it + verb…? ➜ **Does** she cook? No, she doesn't.
Wh-question: What **does** she/he/it + verb…? ➜ What **does** he do? He cooks.

Complete these sentences with the missing verbs from the story on page 39:

My wife _____. She _____ at home and _____ the kids.
She _____ to cook and read.
My older son _____ to school. He _____ to play video games.
My younger son _____ to learn letters and numbers.

Look closely at the verbs in the third person singular*:

My wife stay**s** at home. She **doesn't** work. She watch**es** the children.
She like**s** to cook and read. She **doesn't** like to watch TV.
My older son go**es** to school. My younger son **does not** go to school.

*The third person singular ➜ she/he/it (it = impersonal pronoun)
      The first person singular ➜ I
      The second person singular and plural ➜ you
      The first person plural ➜ we
      The third person plural ➜ they

Follow how to change verbs to the third person singular:

- Add the suffix "-s/-es" to the verbs:
  work ➜ work**s**; stay ➜ stay**s**; watch ➜ watch**es**; do ➜ do**es**; go ➜ go**es**
- Say the suffix "-s" ➜ /s/ after the voiceless consonants:
  work**s**/s/, get**s**/s/, celebrate**s**/s/
- Say the suffix "-s/es" ➜ /z/ after the vowels and voiced consonants:
  see**s**/z/, play**s**/z/, drive**s**/z/, tell**s**/z/, do**es** /dʌz/, go**es** /goʊz/
- Say the suffix "-es" ➜ /ɪz/ after the letters: "ss" "sh" "ch" "x" "z":
  kiss**es**/ɪz/, wash**es**/ɪz/, watch**es**/ɪz/
- Change the letter "y" ➜ "ie":
  carry ➜ carr**ies**/z/, worry ➜ worr**ies**/z/, marry ➜ marr**ies**/z/

How to form negative sentences in the **third person singular**?

Affirmative sentence: She/He/It + verb**s/es**… ➜ Negative sentence: She/He/It **does not** (**doesn't**) + verb (base form)…

1. She drive**s** a ↘car. ➜ She ↘**doesn't** drive a truck.
2. He work**s** from ↘home. ➜ He **does** ↘**not** work at the office.
3. It often ↘rain**s** here. ➜ It ↘**doesn't** often rain there.

Correct the following statements according to the story on page 39. Rewrite them:

1. The husband doesn't work. _____
2. He stays at home and watches his kids. _____
3. His wife works. _____
4. His older son doesn't go to school. _____
5. His younger son goes to school. _____
6. His older son likes to learn letters and numbers. _____
7. His younger son likes to play video games. _____

How well do you know the family from the story? Answer these questions:

1. Does the husband work? _____
2. Does the wife work? _____
3. What does she do at home? _____
4. Does their older son go to school? _____

5. What does he like to play? _____

6. Does their younger son go to school? _____

7. What does he like to learn? _____

8. Do they always celebrate their birthdays? _____

How to ask and answer questions in the **third person singular**?

Affirmative sentence: She/He/It + verb**s/es**… ➔ Yes/No question: **Does** she/he/it + verb (base form)…? Yes, she/he/it **does.**/No, she/he/it **doesn't**…
➔ Wh-question: What **does** she/he/it + verb (base form)…? She/He/It + verb**s/es**…

1. **Does** she ↗work? ↘**Yes**, she ↘**does.**/↘**No**, she **does** ↘**not (doesn't).**
2. **Does** he go to ↗school or **does** he stay ↘home? He go**es** to ↘school.
3. What **do**es he like to ↘do? He like**s** to learn English ↘letters.
4. **Does** it ↗often rain here? ↘Yes, it ↘does./↘No, it ↘doesn't.
5. How often **does** it ↘rain here? It rain**s** ↘often here.

Learn these new wh-words (question words). **Write their translations in this table**:

Question words (wh-words)	Translations
1. Who /hu/	1. _____
2. Which /wɪʧ/ (which of)	2. _____
3. Where /wɛr/	3. _____
4. When /wɛn/	4. _____
5. Why /waɪ/	5. _____
6. Whose /huz/	6. _____
7. How /haʊ/	7. _____

Answer the following wh-questions about the family from the story on page 39. Use the words in parentheses if you need help:

1. Who* works** in the family? (the husband) _____

2. Where does he work? (at an advertising agency) _____

3. Who doesn't work? (the wife) _____

4. Why doesn't she work? (because she watches the kids) _____

5. Which one of their sons goes to school? (the older son) _____

6. Which one of their sons doesn't go to school? (the younger son) _____

7.   How often do they celebrate birthdays? (always) _____

(*No helping verb 'do' when we ask about the subject with the question words 'who' or 'what' and **the main verb ➔ always in the third person singular.)

3. Words

Words	Letters	Sounds
Birthday, three, third, with	"th"	/θ/: interdental, voiceless consonant
Home, he, his, him, her; but: *honest, honor	"h" *silent "h"	/h/: aspirated fricative* voiceless consonant
She, short, sunshine, option, commercial, chef, mission; sure, sugar	"sh" "t" "c" "ch" "ss" "s"	/ʃ/: voiceless fricative consonant (air passes through the top of the mouth, the tip of the tongue is up)
Does, love, come, but, cut, truck, company	"o" "u"	/ʌ/: mid-central, neutral, relaxed (in stressed syllables)
The, a/an, open, agree, prefer, honest, honor	"a" "e" "y" "o" "u" "i"	/ə/: (schwa) mid-central, neutral, relaxed (in unstressed syllables)

*Fricative consonants: voiceless (/h/–/θ/–/ʃ/–/s/–/f/) and voiced (/ð/–/ʒ/–/z/–/v/) ➔ form the continuous friction of the air: /hhh θθθ ʃʃʃ sss fff ððð ʒʒʒ zzz vvv/.

Read these words with the fricative consonants:

/s/–"s": surprise, speak, six, seven, sale, sell, see, smoke, subject, step
/f/–"f": free, fresh, frame, fruit, French, fries, front, fraction, friend /frɛnd/
/ʒ/–"s": usual, usually, vision, visual, Asia, leisure /'liʒɚ/, casual, decision
/z/–"z" "s": zoom, zone, zipper, zoo, zebra, zigzag, lazy, laser, daisy
/v/–"v": van, voice, vase, vacuum, victory, vote, drive, wave, volleyball

Letters ➔ sounds:

Letters "th" ➔ sound /ð/ or /θ/
Letter "h" ➔ sound /h/
Letters "sh" "ch" "c" "ss" "t" "s" ➔ sound /ʃ/
Letters "o" "u"➔ sound /ʌ/ in stressed syllables
All vowel letters in unstressed syllables ➔ sound /ə/ (the schwa sound)

Group the words from the box by the sounds given below:

> Home, he, with, she, his, her, thank, shine, a'gree, does, think, math, come, 'welcome, 'seven, 'company, short, ob'serve, but, sure, 'option, chef, breath

/θ/: _____
/h/: _____
/ʃ/: _____
/ʌ/: _____
/ə/: _____

Sounds → words:
- voiceless fricative consonants: **/h/, /θ/, /ʃ/**
- neutral relaxed vowels: **/ʌ/, /ə/**

1. Consonant /h/ (like breathing out through the mouth) → the letter "h": **h**ello, **h**ome, **h**e, **h**is, **h**er, **h**im, **h**ospital, **h**otel

Read the following words with the initial sound /h/:

> Hero, humor, hope, help, have, hook, hurt, hat, hand, hide, heal, hot, hole, how

> **Note:** the letter "h" → silent:
> - in words: honest, ghost, rhyme, John, vehicle, etc.
> - in wh-words: what, which, where, when, why, whether /'wɛðɚ/...

Read the wh-words with the non-silent sound /h/ only:

> Who, what, which, where, when, why, whose, how

2. Consonant /θ/ (place the tip of the tongue between the teeth and say /sssss/) → the letters "th": **th**ree, **th**ink, **th**in, **th**ick, brea**th**, wi**th**, **th**ank, ba**th**, ma**th**, too**th**, tee**th**

/θ/

Information:

Most words with /θ/ ➔ content words:
- nouns (throat, thorn)
- verbs (think, throw)
- adjectives (thin, thick) and adverbs (thinly, thickly)

Most words with /ð/ ➔ function words:
- article 'the'
- pronouns (they, them, this, that, etc.)
- conjunctions (although), prepositions (within, without; **but**: wi**th**/θ/), etc.

Compare the words with the sounds /ð/ and /θ/ and read them:

/ð/	/θ/
The, they, their, them, this, that, these, those, then, there, though	Thank, think, three, throat, throne, thorn, thread, throw, thaw, theater

3. Consonant /ʃ/ (above the upper teeth) ➔ the letters "sh": **sh**e, **sh**ort, **sh**op, **sh**ip, **sh**ade, wa**sh**, **sh**ampoo, fla**sh**, ca**sh**; "ch": **Ch**icago, **ch**ef; "t": pa**t**ient, na**t**ion, etc.

Read the following words with the sound /ʃ/:

Shell, shed, shake, shirt, skirt, chef, sugar, sure, option, patient, Chicago

Compare these words with the sounds /ʃ/, /tʃ/, /θ/, and /ð/ and read them by row:

/ʃ/	/tʃ/	/θ/	/ð/
She	Chat	Thank	That
Shine	Charm	Think	This
Shape	Chess	Thirsty	Though
Shade	Cheese	Thirst	They
Chef	Chase	Three	Them
Mission	Chair	Thirty	Whether

4. Vowel /ʌ/ (like short and closed /a/) ➔ the letters "u" "o"
- in closed syllables: **c**ut, **f**un, **g**ut, **m**ud, **b**ud, **s**on, **s**un, **st**uff, **u**ncle, **l**uck

- in open syllables: l**o**ve, c**o**me, s**o**me, gl**o**ve, sh**o**ve
- in stressed syllables: ′c**o**mpany, ′m**o**ney, ′**o**ther, an**o**ther, **u**nder, m**o**ther, br**o**ther, c**o**untry, c**o**untryside, g**o**vernment, **u**gly, be′c**au**se

/ʌ/ /ə/

5. Vowel /ə/ (schwa) (like quick and relaxed /ʌ/) ➔ all the vowel letters in **unstressed** syllables: **a**, **a**n, th**e**, **a**′bout, **a**′nother, be′gin, ma′chine, ma′terial, ′**o**pen, ′list**e**n, ′giv**e**n, com′bine, c**o**mpare, p**o**lite, welc**o**me, pers**o**n, c**o**mmand /kə′mænd/

The schwa /ʃwɑ/ sound:
1. Vowel: mid-central, quick, relaxed
2. Phonetic symbol: /ə/ for most vowels in unstressed positions
3. Important vowel (it allows to speak faster and naturally by reducing all the full vowels to /ə/ in unstressed syllables)
4. Typical of American English
5. Present in unstressed syllables in two or more syllable words, generally in the first and/or last syllables of the words:
   A′meric**a**, b**a**′nan**a**, **a**bout, gall**o**n, diffic**u**lt, foc**u**s, hab**i**t, syst**e**m, decim**a**l, pr**o**fession, rem**e**mber, d**e**pressi**o**n, plur**a**l, **a**gain /ə′gɛn/, t**o**′day, t**o**′gether, t**o**′morrow, t**o**′night

Compare the sounds /ʌ/ and /ə/ in the same words and read them:

/ə/	/ʌ/
Another, en**o**ugh /ə′nʌf/, husb**a**nd, muffin, g**o**vernment, ultim**a**te	An**o**ther, en**ou**gh, h**u**sband, m**u**ffin, gov**e**rnment, **u**ltimate

Highlight the words with the sound /ʌ/ in these sentences:

1. I like to study English.
2. My son likes to study numbers.
3. We do fun stuff on Sundays but not on Mondays.
4. My brother sometimes comes on Sundays.
5. Then my son runs around with his uncle. But they don't rush. They have fun.

Study the days of the week (weekdays):

'Sunday, Monday, Tuesday, Wednesday, Thursday, Friday, Saturday
Sunday = the day of the Sun
Monday = the day of the Moon
Saturday = the day of Saturn

(**Note**: bold typed "**s**" ➔ /z/; 'day' ➔ /deɪ/; Wednesday ➔ /ˈwɛnzdeɪ/ (the letters "d" and the second letter "e"– silent)

Letters ➔ words: A B C D E F

Write as many words as you remember with the first six letters of the alphabet:

A: agree, _____
B: birthday, _____
C: compare, _____
D: dream, _____
E: expensive, _____
F: frequent, _____

Numbers:
- cardinal
- ordinal

Study the cardinal numbers.

1-10: One /wʌn/, two /tu/, three /θri/, four /fɔr/, five, six, seven, eight /eɪt/, nine, ten
11-19: E'leven, 'twelve, ˌthir'**teen**, four**teen**, fif**teen**, six**teen**, seven**teen**, eigh**teen**, nine**teen**
Note: many words have two stresses: primary /ˈ/ and secondary /ˌ/: ˌfour'**teen**, 'alˌways, 'someˌtimes, ˌal'ready…
20-100: 'Twenty, 'thirty, forty, fifty, sixty, seventy, eighty, ninety, one hundred, two hundred, three hundred…
Information: **no** "s" at the end of: hundred, thousand, million, billion, trillion ➔ with the exact numbers. For example: five thousand, three million, four hundred
But: hundreds, thousands, millions, billions ➔ approximate number. For example: Hundreds of viewers. Thousands watched this video.

Calculate the sums of the following numbers:

20 + 1 = twenty plus one equals twenty one.
30 + 2 = _____
40 + 4 = _____
60 + 3 = _____
90 + 7 = _____

Do the following subtraction problems:

50 - 8 = fifty minus eight equals forty two
80 - 5 = _____
100 - 11 = _____
5000 - 20 = _____

Observe the changes from cardinal to ordinal numbers:

- change: one ➜ first (1st); two ➜ second (2nd); three ➜ third (3d); twenty-first, thirty-second, forty-third, fifty-first, twenty-second…
- add the suffix '-th' to all other numbers: four + **th** ➜ fourth (4th); five ➜ fifth (5th), six ➜ sixth (6th); nineteen ➜ nineteenth (19th); twen**t**y ➜ twen**ti**e**th** (20th)…

Write the cardinal or ordinal numbers. For example: eleventh – eleven; one – first…

Seventh – _____; five – _____; two – _____
Second – _____; thirteenth – _____; one – _____
Thirty – _____; fortieth – _____; three – _____
Fifteen – _____; fifty – _____; one/a hundred – _____
Third – _____; five hundredth – _____

Articles:
- definite article: **the** /ðə/ or /ði/ (before the vowels)
- indefinite article: **a** /ə/ or **an** /ən/ (before the vowels)

Observe the use of the <u>articles</u> in the following story:

A man comes into a store. He sees a product. The product costs a lot of money. The man thinks. He doesn't like to buy expensive products. The man likes to save money, so he doesn't buy the product. He leaves the store. He saves the money in his wallet.

Discuss the story with the help of these questions:

1. Who comes into the store? Do we know a man who comes into a store?
2. Which store does he come into? Do we know which store he comes into?
3. What product does he see? Do we know what product he sees?
4. What costs a lot of money? Do we know what costs a lot of money?
5. Who thinks? Do we know who thinks?
6. Who likes to save money? Do we know who likes to save money?
7. Who doesn't buy the product? Do we know who doesn't buy the product?

Information: the articles ('a/an' and 'the') define nouns: **a** man ➔ unknown; **the** man ➔ known; **a** product/product**s** ➔ unspecific; **the** product ➔ specific…

How to use the **articles**?

- 'a/an' = any, indefinite ➔ **only** before **singular count** nouns: **a** man, **a** store
- 'the' = someone/something identified or already mentioned in the context ➔ before singular and plural count/noncount nouns: **the** man, **the** stores
- 'the' = someone/something explained: **the** money in his wallet; **the** cat he has
- **no** article ➔ with count nouns in **plural** when we mean people, places, or things in general: a product ➔ products; a man ➔ men; a store ➔ stores
- **no** 'a/an' ➔ with abstract, mass uncountable nouns, which generally don't have plurals: advice, anger, lust, money, happiness, air, nature…
- **no** article ➔ after the phrases: a lot of; a kind of; a piece/pieces of; a bunch of: a lot of books; a bunch of sticks; (the) words of advice…

Explain the use or no use of the indefinite or definite articles in these sentences:

I work as a driver. I drive a truck. I own the truck that I drive. I deliver products. My friend works at an advertising agency. He likes the advertising agency where he works. He provides services.

4. Sentence

Fill in the missing <u>verbs</u> and <u>articles</u> (where necessary) in these sentences:

1. My husband _____ as _____ computer person at _____ advertising company.
2. He _____ _____ company where he works. (like)
3. He _____ _____ van. (drive)

4. He doesn't _____ _____ van. He _____ it. (rent, own)
5. He actually _____ to buy _____ new car. (want)
6. My husband _____ all about _____ cars. (know)

Connect these words into sentences:

celebrate, birthdays, we, always, our _____

like, together, spend, to, we, time _____

wife, cooks, my, usually _____

kids, watch, our, often, videos _____

like, watch, I, TV, to _____

Learn these words:

Family member/members:
- parents /'pɛrənts/: father /'fɑðɚ/, mother /'mʌðɚ/
- child /tʃaɪld/ ➔ children /'tʃɪldrən/: son (boy), daughter /'dɔʈɚ/ (girl)
- siblings: brother, sister
- aunt /ænt//ɑnt/, uncle /ʌnkl/, niece /nis/, nephew /'nɛfju/, cousin /'kʌzn/...

Country/countries:
- the US'A or U'S, 'Canada, 'England, 'Germany, 'India, Ja'pan...

City/cities:
- New York /nu'jɔrk/, London /'lʌndən/, 'Paris, Ber'lin, Moscow /'mɑskaʊ/...

Use the verb 'live' /lɪv/ **and the above words in these sentences**:

I live in _____. My parents and I live in _____.
My father doesn't _____ with us. He _____ in another city.
My mother _____ with me. My children don't _____ with _____. They
_____ in another country.
My daughter _____ in _____. My son _____ in _____.
My aunt _____ in _____. My uncle doesn't _____ in
_____. Their children _____ in _____.

Speak about your own family. Use these questions as a plan for your speech:

1. Where do you live?
2. Do you parents live with you? Where do they live?
3. What does your father do? Where does he work?

4. What does your mother do? Where does she work?
5. Do you have siblings? Where do they live? What do they do?
6. Do you have children? Do they go to school or work?
7. What do they like to do? Where do they like to go?
8. How do you spend time together?

5. Text

Fill in the correct <u>pronouns</u> in the story. Use this table for help:

> I — my — me; you — your — you; she — her — her; he — his — him
> It — its — it; we — our — us; they — their — them

In the picture, _____ see _____ family. You see _____wife, _____ kids, and _____.
_____ wife doesn't work. _____ watches _____ kids. _____ children like to spend
time with _____. They like to celebrate _____ birthdays, so _____ always celebrate
_____ birthdays. And _____ often celebrate _____ birthdays at home.

Write a story about your family. Use these unfinished sentences if you choose:

My family and I live in…
I work as a…
My wife/husband works as a…
My wife/husband…
We have _____/_____ child/children. They…

Write a story about your parents and/or grandparents:

> My parents live…
> My dad…
> My mom…
> My grandparents ("d"– silent)…

Recite the story about your parents and your family.

Homework:
1. Watch the "Sounds American" videos about the sounds: /h/ /θ/ /ʃ/ /ʌ/ /ə/.
2. Look up more information about the English articles (in your first language).

Lesson 5

Text: **Today and Yesterday**
Affirmatives, negatives, and questions with '**did**' (Past Simple tense):
- I/You/She/He/It/We/They + verb (past tense form)…
- I/You/She/He/It/We/They **didn't (did not)** + verb…
- **Did** I/you/she/he/it/we/they + verb…?
- What **did** I/you/she/he/we/they/ + verb?

Simple sentences → **compound** and **complex** sentences
Adjectives → adverbs
Words—letters—sounds:
Yesterday—"y"—/j/; thi**ng**/tha**nk**—"ng" "n"—/ŋ/; **j**oke—"j"—/dʒ/

---

1. Text

"Today and Yesterday"

Good Morning!
What do you do every day? What did you do yesterday?

I normally get up early, so my day starts early. I like to follow my daily routines and keep up with my everyday schedule. In the early morning hours, I take a shower, make coffee, and walk outside for about twenty minutes. I listen to podcasts in English while I walk. That helps me learn English. Then I get ready for my job. I usually drive to work.
So yesterday I got up at 4:30 am as usual and today I woke up at the same time. But yesterday I didn't drive to work because my car broke down. I took a bus. After work, I fixed my car and drove to buy groceries. Because I bought food yesterday, I cooked my early dinner today. After dinner, I rested. But I didn't rest yesterday because I worked on my car, as I already mentioned. Naturally, I go to sleep early so that I get up early and do many things in the morning. Then I fall asleep easily and sleep well. Yesterday I went to sleep early and I go to bed now. Good night!

Information: verbs + adverbs/prepositions = **phrasal verbs** with the stress on the second word: get 'up, wake 'up, keep 'up, break 'down, look 'up
Note: always look up the meanings of the phrasal verbs because they don't mean what the verbs mean. For example, 'look' = glance; but 'look up' = find information

Look up the following phrasal verbs from the story:

1. get up = _____
2. wake up = _____
3. keep up = _____
4. break down = _____

Find the opposite pairs. Draw lines to connect them:

Begin	Walk
Buy groceries	Get up
Fix	Take a cab
Take a bus	Work
Rest	Sell groceries
Go to sleep	End
Drive	Break

2. Sentence

Past time ➜ the Past Simple tense ➜ past events and actions
Affirmative sentence: I/You/She/He/It/We/They + verb (**past** form)…
Negative sentence: I/You/She/He/It/We/They **didn't** (**did not**) + verb (**present** form)…
Yes/No question: **Did** I/you/she/he/it/we/they + verb (present form)…?
Wh-question: What **did** I/you/she/he/it/we/they + verb (present form)…?

Observe how the verbs describe present-time and past-time actions:

1. My usual day <u>begins</u> early. Yesterday <u>began</u> early for me too.
2. I normally get up at 4:30 in the morning. And yesterday I got up at 4:30 am.
3. I usually drive to work but yesterday I didn't drive.
4. My car always worked fine. But yesterday for some reason it broke down.
5. I generally don't take a bus but yesterday I took a bus because of that.
6. Every day I walk two miles. Yesterday I walked three miles. Good for me!
7. I buy groceries once a week. I actually bought food yesterday.
8. I go to bed early, so yesterday I again went to sleep early.

Compare the verbs in the present and past tense forms:

Present	Past	Present	Past
get up	got up	buy	bought
wake up	woke up	fix	fixed
take	took	cook	cooked
drive	drove	rest	rested
break	broke	go	went

Write the missing verbs that describe what I did yesterday. Use the verbs in parentheses if necessary:

1. I _____ at 4:30 am.* (get up)
2. I _____ a bus. (take)
3. I _____ my car. (fix)
4. I _____ to buy groceries. (drive)
5. I _____ food. (buy)
6. I _____ my dinner. (cook)
7. I _____ to bed early. (go)

(*am = in the morning; pm = in the afternoon)

How to form verbs in the **Past Simple tense**?

Verbs: regular and irregular
Regular verbs: add -d/-ed ➔ live + d = lived; follow + ed = followed.
Say:
- /t/ after the voiceless consonants:
  fix + ed = fixed /fɪkst/; cook + ed = cooked /kʊkt/; help + ed = helped; work + ed = worked
- /d/ after the voiced consonants and vowel sounds/diphthongs:
  agree + d = agreed; love + d = loved; stay + ed = stayed
- /ɪd/ or /əd/ after the letters "t" or "d":
  rest + ed = rested /'rɛstəd/, hand + ed = handed; test + ed = tested

Change: "y" ➔ "ie": try ➔ tried; study ➔ studied
Double the last consonants: plan ➔ planned, shop ➔ shopped, prefer ➔ preferred

Irregular verbs (exceptions): see a list of some irregular verbs below!

Study and remember some irregular verbs in the following table:

Present	Past	Translation
Become	became	
Begin	began	
Bring	brought	
Choose	chose	
Come	came	
Cut	cut	
Drink	drank	
Eat	ate	
Fall	fell	
Feel	felt	
Find	found	
Fly	flew	
Forgive	forgave	
Get	got	
Give	gave	
Hear	heard	
Hide	hid	
Keep	kept	
Know	knew	
Leave	left	

Write the present tense of these past tense verbs. Insert them correctly in the affirmative and negative sentences below:

Woke up – _____; ate – _____; went – _____; drove – _____; walked – _____; bought – _____; decided – _____; began – _____

1. Today we _____ at 4:30 am. We didn't _____ so early yesterday.
2. We _____ sweet cereal for breakfast yesterday. We didn't _____that today.
3. We _____ to a supermarket yesterday. By the way, we didn't _____ there. We _____.
4. At the supermarket, we _____ fresh fruits and vegetables. We didn't _____ sweet cereal because we _____ to eat fresh fruits and vegetables and get up early from then on. So we _____ a healthy lifestyle.

Compound and complex sentences

Observe the compound and complex sentences from the story on page 52. Circle or underscore the <u>conjunctions</u> in these sentences:

- I normally get up early, so my day starts early.
- I listen to podcasts in English while I walk.
- I didn't drive to work yesterday because my car broke down.
- I didn't rest yesterday because I worked on my car, as I already mentioned.
- I go to sleep early so that I get up early and go for a walk.

Compare these types of sentences:

Simple sentence	Complex sentence (1)	Compound sentence (2)
I get up early.	I get up early, **therefore** I do many things in the morning.	I get up early **and** I make my bed right away.
I took a bus yesterday.	I took a bus **because** my car broke down.	I didn't drive yesterday **yet** I took a bus.
I go to bed early.	I go to bed early **so that** I wake up early.	I go to bed early, **so** I get up early and go to the gym.

(1) Complex sentence ➜ simple sentence + conjunction* + subordinate clause (*conjunctions: after, although, as, because, if, so that, therefore/that's why…)
(2) Compound sentence ➜ simple sentence + conjunction** + simple sentence (**conjunctions: and, but, or, so, yet, for…)

Match the why-questions with the answers based on the story on page 52:

Why-questions	Answers
1. Why do you get up early? 2. Why do you follow your daily routines? 3. Why do you usually drive to work? 4. Why did you take a bus yesterday? 5. Why do you have groceries today? 6. Why do you go to sleep early? 7. Why do you like to start your day early?	• Because I bought food yesterday. • Because I wake up early. • Because I like to keep up with my schedule. • Because my car broke down. • Because a bus takes long. • Because I like to get up early. • Because I want to do many things in the morning.

From the story on page 52, find the sentences that explain why I didn't do the following yesterday. Finish these complex sentences:

- I **didn't** drive yesterday **because** _____
- I **didn't** rest yesterday **because** _____

Complete the sentences with the missing <u>conjunctions</u>. Choose from these conjunctions: after, and, because, but, while, so that, so.

1. I usually wake up at 4:30 am _____ yesterday I woke up at that time.
2. In the morning, I listen to English podcasts _____ I walk.
3. Every day I drive to work _____ yesterday I didn't.
4. I took a bus yesterday _____ my car didn't start.
5. I drove to buy food _____ I fixed my car.
6. I go to sleep early _____ I can get up early.
7. Yesterday I went to bed early, _____ I woke up early today.

Adjectives and adverbs

Adjectives describe <u>nouns</u> (people, things, places, ideas, etc.):
>	open, silent, **daily**, **early**, normal, useful, hopeful, hopeless, useless, uncomfortable, honest, dishonest…

Adverbs describe <u>verbs</u> (and adjectives):
>	openly, silently, **daily**, **early**, normally, usefully, hopefully, hopelessly, uselessly, uncomfortable, honestly, dishonestly…

Distinguish the <u>adjectives</u> and <u>adverbs</u>. Underscore the adjectives and circle the adverbs in these sentences:

> My day begins early. I eat my early dinner.
> I follow my daily schedule. I exercise daily.
> I fall asleep easily. I have an easy task.
> Last night I slept well. It means I had good quality sleep.

Circle the <u>adjectives</u> and underscore the <u>nouns</u> in the following sentences:

1. My dear friend told me interesting things about his everyday life.
2. He shared the important ideas that I liked and wanted to include in my daily life.
3. Every day he does useful and exciting activities.
4. In the morning, he runs long distances.
5. During the day, he works on creative projects.
6. In the afternoon, he cooks yummy meals.
7. In the evening, he reads philosophical books. Wow!

How to form **adjectives**?

1. Add the **suffixes** to nouns or verbs: '-able' '-al' '-ant' '-d/ed' '-ing' '-ful' '-less' '-ous' '-ive'… For example: comfort + able = comfort**able**; norm + al = norm**al**; import + ant = import**ant**; close + d = close**d**; interest + ing = interest**ing**, use + ful = use**ful**; use + less = use**less**; continue + ous = continu**ous**; cooperate + ive = cooperat**ive**…

2. Add the **prefixes** to adjectives: 'il-' 'im-' 'ir-' 'in-' 'dis-' 'un-' ➔ for a negative meaning. For example: legal ➔ **il**legal; polite ➔ **im**polite; regular ➔ **ir**regular; active ➔ **in**active; honest ➔ **dis**honest; forgettable ➔ **un**forgettable...

3. Use adjectives **before** nouns: an **open** door; **unopened** letters; **famous** writers…

How to form **adverbs**?

- Adverbs ➔ adjectives + the suffix '-ly': usual + ly = usual**ly**, nice + ly = nice**ly**, correct + ly = correct**ly**, interesting + ly = interesting**ly**…
- Use adverbs before/after verbs and before adjectives.

Insert the suitable adjectives (wonderful, fresh, delicious, great, se'rene, peaceful, high, unforgettable) **into this context**:

- Last month we had a _____ vacation.
- We went to the countryside and had a _____ time there.
- We enjoyed _____ nature.
- We sat near a _____ lake.
- We climbed a _____ hill.
- We tasted _____, _____ fruits.
- We took many _____ pictures.

Circle the <u>adverbs</u> and underscore the <u>verbs</u> in the following sentences:

I dearly loved my father.
He always treated me lovingly. He never treated me badly.
We regularly did many things together, playfully and interestingly.
Sadly, he recently passed away.
I constantly remember him.

Form adverbs by adding the suffix '-ly' to the adjectives in the table:

Adjectives	Adverbs
1. Creative	1. _____
2. Continuous	2. _____
3. Wonderful	3. _____
4. General	4. _____
5. Comfortable	5. _____
6. Strong	6. _____
7. Bad	7. _____

Look at the exceptions:

Adjectives	Adverbs	Adverbs
Good job!	Work **well**!	
Fast walk	Walk **fast**!	
Hard work	Work **hard**!	Hardly (barely, narrowly)
A **late** call	Don't stay up **late**!	Lately (recently)

Insert the adjectives and the adverbs in parentheses in the correct places.
Rewrite the sentences as a story:

1. My uncle tells stories. (boring, humorously) _____
2. After he got married, his wife and he went on a trip to visit her parents. (shortly, short, elderly) _____
3. Her parents lived in a town far from a city. (retired, always, small, big) _____

_____

4. My uncle drove a(an) car. (still, old-fashioned) _____
5. The car stopped. (unsurprisingly, unreliable, suddenly) _____

_____

6. My uncle said to his wife, "Honey, we arrived at our destination." (funny, calmly, young, just, final) _____
7. They didn't panic but went for a walk around. (helplessly, quietly, nice) _____

_____

8. When they returned to their car, it started. (abandoned, miraculously) _____

_____

3. Words

Words	Letters	Sounds
Morni**ng**, eveni**ng**, thi**ng**, lo**ng**, goi**ng**, tha**nk**, pi**nk**	ending "ng" "n" followed by "k" "g"	/ŋ/: nasal consonant, the tongue touches the soft palate at the back
Yesterday, **y**es, **y**oung, **u**se	"y" "u"	/j/ /ju/: voiced consonant
Job, pro**j**ect, **j**uice, **g**eneral, ba**dg**e, **j**u**dg**e, sche**d**ule, indivi**d**ual	"j" "g" "dg" "d" followed by "u"	/dʒ/: voiced, alveolar consonant

Letters ➔ sounds:

- the letter "n" before the letters "k" "g"; the letters "ng" at the end of words ➔ sound /ŋ/
- the letter "y" ➔ sound /j/
- the letters "j" "g" "d" "dg" ➔ sound /dʒ/

Circle the letters that give the consonant sounds /ŋ/, /j/, /dʒ/ in these words:

/ŋ/: ta**n**k, ri**ng**, 'everythi**ng**, langua**n**ge, anythi**ng**, si**ng**, so**ng**, tru**n**k, ba**n**k, stro**ng**
/j/: **y**ellow, comp**u**ter, **y**ou, **U**nited States, **y**ogurt, **y**oga, New **Y**ork, **u**se, **u**niform
/dʒ/: **j**ust, e**d**ucation, **g**eneration, drink, pa**g**e, **j**og, mana**g**e, **j**u**dg**ment, langua**g**e

Sounds ➔ words:

- consonants: **/ŋ/, /j/, /dʒ/**

1. Consonant /ŋ/ ➔ the letter "n" before "k" "g": tha**n**k, ta**n**k, E**n**glish, la**n**guage; the letters "ng" at the end of the words: morni**ng**, eveni**ng**, thi**ng**, stro**ng**, bori**ng**, lovi**ng**...

Read and remember these imperative sentences:

- In the morning, sing a song!
- In the evening, say "Thank you!"
- Speak the English language in England all day long!
- Don't do the wrong /rɔŋ/ things!
- Play ping-pong every /'ɛvri/ evening!
- Take everything, something, anything, nothing!

Compare the /ŋ/ and /n/ consonants. Read these minimal pairs:

Bang — ban; king — kin; ping — pin; sing — sin; thing — thin; wing — win

2. Consonant /j/ ➔ the letters "y" "u": **y**ou, **y**our, **y**oung, **y**ellow, **y**oga, **y**ogi, **u**sual, **u**seful, h**u**man, h**u**mor, **u**se, document, comp**u**ter

Read the following words with the sound /j/:

Youth, figure, unique, unit, unite, younger, yard, yacht /jɑt/, yell, yawn, yummy

3. Consonant /dʒ/ ➔ the letters "j" "g" "dg": mana**g**e, bu**dg**et, **j**oke; the letter "d" before the letter "u": sche**d**ule /'skɛdʒəl/, indivi**d**ual, di**d** you

Read the following words with the sound /dʒ/:

Angel, message, journalist, surgery, vegetable, vegetarian, page, arrangement, orange, storage, gentleman, gym, ginger, gadget, bridge, fridge, schedule, joke

Read this joke. Explain why Ben got an 'A' and Tom got an 'F.'

A teacher called two students to her desk.
She said: "You both answered the questions correctly, but Ben got an 'A' and Tom got an 'F.'
Tom protested: "Why didn't I get an 'A' if we both answered the questions correctly?"
"Because," the teacher explained, "where Ben wrote, 'I don't know,' you wrote, 'I don't know either.'

(**Note**: the word 'either' = 'too' (also) in negative sentences.)

Read 'did you' **as** /dɪ'dʒu/ **and** 'didn't you' **as** /dɪdn'tʃju/ **in the following questions**:

1. Did you figure out* why Tom got an 'F'?
2. What did you just say to me?
3. Where did you go yesterday?
4. Why didn't** you call me yesterday?
5. Didn't you know my younger son?
6. Did you try to contact the management?
7. Why didn't you email them on time?

(*figure out /fɪgjɚ'aʊt/ = understand; **the letter "t" ➔ /tʃ/ followed by "u": pic**t**ure…)

Compare the voiced /dʒ/ and voiceless /tʃ/ consonants in these minimal pairs:

Badge — batch; junk — chunk; jeep — cheap; ridge — rich; jest — chest

Letters ➔ words: G H I J K L

Write as many words as you remember with the next six letters of the alphabet:

G: generally, _____
H: humor, _____
I: ideal, _____
J: joke, _____
K: know, _____
L: lovely, _____

4. Sentence

Learn these phrases that describe usual routines:

Morning rituals:
make one's bed = _____
brush one's teeth = _____
exercise/do morning exercises = _____
get dressed = _____
put on makeup = _____
make a cup of hot tea/coffee = _____
have/eat breakfast = _____

Household chores:
wash (the) dishes/wash up = _____
vacuum the floor/carpet/rug = _____
do (the) laundry = _____
fold/iron/hang (the) clothes _____
shop for groceries/go or do grocery shopping _____
cook/make/prepare/fix lunch _____

Evening activities:
hang out/go out with a spouse/family _____
eat out/eat in _____
catch up on the day _____
go out to walk/go for a walk _____
watch/see a movie _____
chat on the phone/email/text/message _____

Describe your usual and yesterday activities. Use the above-mentioned phrases.
Follow this scenario:

Every day I _____.
But I don't _____ every day.
I _____ only weekly (monthly).
Yesterday I _____.
I also _____.
And I didn't _____.
But I plan to _____.
I wanted to _____ but I didn't _____.

Connect these simple sentences into compound and complex sentences. Choose from the conjunctions in parentheses:

1. I make my bed. I get up. (after/as soon as)
2. I don't exercise in the morning. I exercise in the evening. (but/however)
3. It takes me a long time to get dressed. I put on makeup and iron my clothes. (because/as)
4. I don't like to wash dishes. I like to vacuum and do laundry. (but/however)
5. I don't shop for groceries. I order food online. (because/since)
6. In the evening, we hang out together. We catch up on our day. (and/so that)
7. We don't eat out frequently. We prefer to eat in. (as/because)

Ask your friend about her/his last weekend and write down her/his answers. Ask the questions with these wh-question words:

What… \
When… \
What time… \
Where… \
How… \
How long… \
Why…

5. Text

Share your daily schedule. Write in your everyday activities according to the parts of the day. Remember the details of your yesterday activities:

Parts of the day:	Every day:	Yesterday:
In the morning,		
In the afternoon,		
In the evening,		

Speak about your usual and yesterday routines. Use these questions to help you:

1. How early do you go to sleep? What time did you go to bed yesterday?
2. What do you usually do in the morning? What did you do yesterday morning?
3. Do you go out for a walk every day? Did you go out yesterday?
4. How do you get to work? Do you drive or do you take a bus?
5. What do you normally do in the evening? What did you do yesterday evening?

Write a report about your daily and yesterday activities:

Daily activities (What I usually do)	Yesterday activities (What I did yesterday)

Tell us about your last vacation. Use these questions if necessary:

- When did you go on vacation last time?
- Did you travel anywhere?
- Why did you choose that place for your vacation?
- What did you do there?
- How long did you stay there?
- How did you like your last vacation?
- Did anything unpredictable happen during your vacation?

Compare what you did last year and what you do this year. Write in this table:

Last year	This year

Homework:
1. Watch the "Sounds American" videos that practice the consonants: /ŋ/, /j/, /dʒ/.
2. Look up more information about the Past Simple tense.
3. Find a table of irregular verbs and continue studying them.

Lesson 6

Text: **Today and Tomorrow**

Affirmatives, negatives, and questions with the verb 'will' (Future Simple tense):
- I/You/She/He/It/We/They **will** + verb…
- I/You/She/He/It/We/They **won't (will not)** + verb…
- **Will** I/you/she/he/it/we/they + verb…?
- What **will** I/you/she/he/it/we/they + verb…?

Simple sentences ➔ **conditional** sentences

Adjectives/adverbs: **comparative—superlative** ➔ good/well—better—best

Words—letters—sounds:

Will—"ll"—/ɬ/; better/water—"tt" "t"—/t̬/; impor**tant**—"tan"—/?n/; li**sten**—"sten"—/sn/

---

1. Text

"Today and Tomorrow"

Hi there! I have something for you to think about. Don't we do today what we did yesterday, and tomorrow we will do what we do today? Today I continue to do what I did yesterday. Tomorrow I will continue doing what I do today. I started a new project yesterday. Today I picked up where I left off yesterday. And tomorrow I will resume the project. If I do my best today, I will move closer to success. I will successfully complete the project if I work harder and smarter today. How will I succeed? Firstly, I will set my goal. Secondly, I will plan the steps toward my goal. Based on my progress today, I will project how to progress tomorrow. What do you think of this strategy? How do you work today on making your future better?

Learn the following words, phrasal verbs, and phrases:

1. continue to do/continue doing or continue something = keep up, go on, carry on
2. pick up = resume, continue, start again (also: go to get someone or something)
3. leave off = stop, discontinue
4. do one's best = try hard, make every effort, make efforts
5. set a goal/goals = decide what to achieve
6. work on = spend time advancing, influence
7. make better = improve

Mind the change of word stress in these nouns and verbs. Read them with the correct word stress in the sentences below:

- a project /ˈprɑdʒəkt/ — to project /prəˈdʒɛkt/
- progress /ˈprɑgrəs/ — to progress /prəˈgrɛs/
  But: success /səkˈsɛs/ — to succeed /səkˈsid/

I started a new project yesterday. Tomorrow I will resume the project.
Based on my progress today, I will project how to progress tomorrow.

Match the synonyms. Draw lines to connect them:

Complete	Discontinue
Improve	Finish
Leave off	Plan
Project	Achieve
Progress	Pick up
Resume	Develop better
Succeed	Move forward

2. Sentence

Future time → the Future Simple tense → future events and actions

Affirmatives: I/You/She/He/It/We/They **will** + verb…
Negatives: I/You/She/He/It/We/They **won't (will not)** + verb…
Yes/no questions: **Will** I/you/she/he/it/we/they + verb…?
Wh-questions: What **will** I/you/she/he/it/we/they + verb…?

Sort out the <u>verbs</u> in these sentences that refer to the past, present, and future. Write them down below:

1. We do today what we did yesterday, and tomorrow we will do what we did today.
2. I started a new project yesterday. Today I continue. Tomorrow I will resume it.
3. I study English. Yesterday I studied English and I will study English tomorrow.
4. I drive to work. I drove to work yesterday and tomorrow I will also drive to work.
5. We celebrate our birthdays. We celebrated them last year. We will celebrate them next year.

- Past tense: _____
- Present tense: _____
- Future tense: _____

Compare the verbs in the past, present, and future tenses:

I **went** to school. I **go** to school Monday through Friday. I **will go** to school again.
I **read** /rɛd/ many books. I **read** books every day. I **will read** books in the future.
I **worked** hard. I **work** hard. I **will work** hard.

Rewrite the present tense sentences in the past tense and future tense:

I did (past tense) ➔ I do (present tense) ➔ I will do (future tense)

1. _____. I learn English. _____.
2. _____. You need to work hard. _____.
3. _____. She works smart. _____.
4. _____. He knows his duty. _____.
5. _____. We gradually progress. _____.
6. _____. They set their goals. _____.

How to form the Future Simple tense?

Affirmative: I **will** succeed. (I'**ll** succeed.)
Negative: I **will not** (**won't**) fail.
Yes/No question: **Will** I succeed? Yes, I **will**.
Wh-question: What **will** I achieve?

1. They'll come ↘soon. We will ↘wait for them.
2. I will ↘not go there. I ↘won't go there.
3. Will you ↗help me? Yes, I will. (No, I won't.)
4. When will you ↘help me? What will you do to ↘morrow?
5. How will I suc↘ceed?
   ↗Firstly, I will set my ↘goal.
   ↗Secondly, I will plan the ↘steps toward my goal.
   ↗Thirdly, I will ↘regularly project how to progress each day.

Conditional sentences

I will do my best. + I will move closer to success. ➔ **If I do** my best, **I will move** closer to success. **I'll move** closer to success **if I do** my best.

How to form **conditional** sentences?

1. **If** I/you/she/he/it/we/they + **verb**…, I//you/she/he/it/we/they **will** + verb…
2. I/You/She/He/We/They **will** + verb… **if** I/you/she/he/it/we/they + **verb**…

1. **If I work** harder and smarter today, I **will** successfully complete the project.
2. I **will** successfully complete the project if I **work** harder and smarter today.

No helping verb "will" in **if**-clauses of conditional sentences as well as in **time** clauses with the conjunctions: when, until, unless, as soon as, after, before…
Use "will" only in main clauses: I **will** succeed **if I work** hard and smart.

Highlight the conditional and time clauses in these complex sentences:

1. We'll be late if you don't hurry up.
2. We won't achieve our goals unless we work hard.
3. Will you help me if I ask you to*?
4. I'll text you when I get home.
5. As soon as I get home, I'll call you.
6. Please call me after you speak with your boss!
7. Will you listen to me before you make your decision?

(*to = the unfinished verb in the infinitive)

Complete these sentences with the correct forms of the verbs of your choice in parentheses:

I will help you if you _____ (not mind/agree).
I'll drive her home if she _____ (need to/want me to).
We'll wait for you until you _____ (come back home/get back to us).
If you don't lose hope, you _____ (win/see the result).
When we believe in our dreams, they _____ (come true/materialize).
She will become a great teacher if she _____ (believe so/think so).
We will wait patiently until the things _____ (clear up/make sense).

Connect these simple sentences into conditional and time sentences:

- My dreams will come true. I will work on them. _____
- I will pass the test. I'll study hard. _____
- We'll see you tonight. You will visit us. _____
- I will call you. You will pick me up. _____
- She will catch the first bus. She'll get up early. _____
- My mom will retire soon. She'll travel the world. _____
- He will finish the project. He will do his best. _____
- Her friend will help her. She will manage. _____

Finish these sentences with your own ideas:

1. He'll understand you if _____
2. You will sleep well if _____
3. We'll help you as soon as _____
4. My parents will visit me when _____
5. I won't look for a new job until _____
6. My friend will call me in case _____
7. She will explain the problem after _____

3. Words

Words	Letters	Sounds
Better, beautiful, exciting, later, water, matter, letter little, battle, party, forty	"t" "tt"	flap /t̬/ (like quick /d/): between the vowels or vowels and the consonants "l" and "r"
Important, mitten, mountain, fountain, written, pattern	"t" "tt"	/ʔ/ (glottal stop), no /ə/ between /t/ and /n/; /t/ + /n/ → /ʔn/
Listen, fasten, Christmas, castle, exactly, soften	silent "t"	/sn/: no sound /t/ after the letters: "s" "c" "f"
Look, listen, love, like, love, leaf, leave, live, hello, along Will, people, battle, really, all, early, daily, well	"l" "ll" / "ll" "l"	/l/ : "light" → at the beginning of words or syllables /ɫ/: "dark" → in the middle and at the end of words or syllables

Letters → sounds:

- the letter "t" → flap /t̬/
- the letter "t" → /ʔ/ (glottal stop)
- the letter "t" → silent
- the letter "l" → light /l/ or dark /ɫ/

Syllables with a consonant + le:

In syllables with a consonant + le, the middle vowel remains short as in closed syllables and the last letter "e" → silent: little, handle, puzzle

Learn the poem "Little Things" (by Julia Abigail Fletcher Carney, American poet):

> *"Little drops of water*
> *Little grains of sand,*
> *Make the mighty ocean,*
> *And the pleasant land.*
>
> *Little deeds of kindness,*
> *Little words of love,*
> *Make our Earth an Eden,*
> *Like the heaven above."*

Remember these interesting phrases and words from the poem:

drops of water = _____
grains of sand = _____
deeds of kindness = _____
words of love = _____
mighty, pleasant, heaven /ˈhɛvən/...

Sounds → words:

- flap /t̬/ (like quick, soft /d/; glottal stop /ʔ/; silent
- light /l/ (alveolar); dark /ɫ/ (in the back of the mouth)

Sort out these words in three groups and write them down below:

Get up, curtain, little, daughter, thirty, Manhattan, city, Christmas, moisten, later, dirty, whistle (silent "h"), pattern, wrestle (silent "w"), matter, kitten, forgotten, whatever, got to go, got it, important, water, better, fasten, party, matter, soften

- flap /t̬/: _____
- glottal stop /ʔ/: _____
- silent "t": _____

Read these words with the letter "t" correctly as: the alveolar sound /t/, flap /t̬/, glottal stop /ʔ/, and the silent letter "t":

/t/: television, toward /ˈtɔə-d/, talk, teach, take, time, tell, team, itinerary, Italian
/t̬/: auto, motto, better, beauty, computer, data, pretty, bottle, party, thirty, water
/ʔ/: accountant, cotton, important, frighten, Latin, certain, button, mountain
Silent "t": listen, watch, match, whistle, often, mostly, lastly, exactly, soften, softly

Sort out the words given below between:

- the light /l/: _____
- the dark /ɫ/: _____

Will, long, help, pool, learn, flag, really, table, look, letter, family, please, all, last ball, people, golf, love, like, leaf, early, usually, leave, live, hello, along, able

Read these words with the dark /ɫ/ by pulling the tongue back into the mouth:

All, pull, bill, goal, college, email, family, model, role, tall, always, people, please, really, generally, fabulously, beautifully, normally

Read the words with the sound /r/ and the sounds /l/ and /ɫ/:

Try – fly; pray – play; praise – place; firing – filing; fearing – feeling

Read these words with the sounds /r/ and /ɫ/:

Early, literally, squirrel /ˈskwɜ-əl/, world, girl, fragile /ˈfrædʒəl/, wrinkle (silent "w")

Letters → words: M N O P Q R S

Write as many words as you remember with the next seven letters of the alphabet:

M: _____
N: _____

O: _____

P: _____

Q: _____

R: _____

S: _____

4. Sentence

Choose the phrases of time from this table and use them in the sentences below:

Past	Present	Future
Yesterday, the day before yesterday, the other day Last night, last weekend, last year, last winter, last century, past week Two weeks later, a month later, ten years later A year ago, two days ago, a minute ago	Daily, weekly, monthly, yearly, every year, every evening, every Saturday This week, this weekend, this month, this year On Sunday(s)… In the mornings… Once a day, twice a month, three times a year	Tomorrow, the day after tomorrow, the next day, tonight, soon, eventually, immediately (the) next week, next month, next year, next weekend Next Monday/Sunday… the upcoming week, the following year In a minute, in a month, in a day, in a year

1. Every _____ I get up early but _____ I woke up late.
2. Last _____ I worked on my assignment for the next _____.
3. I'll continue working on this project _____ because I need to finish it by next _____.
4. I will start my new job in a _____.
5. If I complete this work by _____, I'll rest this _____.
6. That happened many _____ ago.
7. After I left the office, the boss called me _____ later.
8. I'll go on vacation _____. I will be back at work _____.
9. We go to the gym _____ a week. We like to work out in the _____.

73

Rewrite the following sentences with the adverbs in parentheses:

- (usually, occasionally) I exercise in the morning but I work out in the evening. _____

- (frequently, carefully) We eat out, so we choose restaurants where we go.

  _____

- (amazingly, eventually) Once I sang this song but I forgot the lyrics.

  _____

- (fluently, accurately) I speak English but I also want to speak it.

  _____

- (finally, happily) We got the news that our boss will retire from their job.

  _____

Adjectives and adverbs:
- comparatives
- superlatives

Identify the parts of speech of the words "best, closer, harder, smarter, better" **in these sentences**:

1. If I do my best today, I will move closer to success.
2. I will successfully complete the project if I work harder and smarter today.
3. I believe in my better future.

Check your answers:
- do my best ➔ verb + noun
- work harder and smarter ➔ verb + adverb
- better future ➔ adjective + noun

Compare the qualities of things and actions. Highlight the comparative adjectives and adverbs in the following sentences:

1. We drive a nice car but our neighbor drives a nicer car.
2. I work very hard but my coworker works even harder than me.
3. My brother gets up early but I get up earlier than him.
4. All students in my class speak better English now.
5. This person talks fast. However, I speak faster.

How do adjectives become comparative and superlative?

Base form	Comparative: '-er'/'more' (than)	Superlative: '-est'/'most'
good	**better**	the **best**
close	closer	the closest
hard	harder	the hardest
smart	smarter	the smartest
fast	faster	the fastest
bad	**worse**	the **worst**
little	**less**	the **least**
old	older	the oldest
young	younger	the youngest
bi**g**	bi**gg**er	the bi**gg**est
slow	slower	the slowest
pretty	prettier	the prettiest
many	more	(the) most
clear	clearer/more clear	the clearest/most clear
happy	happier	the happiest
beautiful	more beautiful	the most beautiful
exciting	more exciting	the most exciting
thrilling	more thrilling	the most thrilling

Write the base forms for the comparatives and superlatives of these adjectives:

_____ – better – best; _____ – worse – worst; _____ – less – least
_____ – fast – faster; _____ – harder – hardest; _____ – more – most
_____ – more clear – the most clear; _____ – prettier – the prettiest
_____ – more thrilling – most thrilling; _____ – happy – the happiest

Insert the correct forms of the adjectives (in parentheses) into these sentences:

1. Last summer my sister had the _____vacation ever. (wonderful)
2. She plans a _____ vacation next year than the last year. (awesome)
3. This year my brother has a _____ job than last year. (interesting)
4. The new job also pays him a _____ salary than the previous one. (big)
5. Now he feels the _____ because he wants to buy a _____ house than the present one. (happy, spacious)

How do adverbs become comparative and superlative?

Base form	Comparative: '-er'/'more' (than)	Superlative: '-est'/'most'
well	**better**	**best**
close/closely	more closely	most closely
hard	harder	hardest
fast	faster	fastest
late	later	latest
badly	**worse**	**worst**
little	**less**	**least**
early	earlier	earliest
slowly	more slowly	most slowly
clear/clearly	more clearly	most clearly
happily	more happily	most happily
fluently	more fluently	most fluently
frequently	more frequently	most frequently
beautifully	more beautifully	most beautifully
excitingly	more excitingly	most excitingly
gracefully	more gracefully	most gracefully

Write the base forms for the comparatives and superlatives of these adverbs:

_____ – better – best; _____ – worse – worst; _____ – later – latest
_____ – earlier – earliest: _____ – more frequently – most frequently
_____ – more accurately – most accurately

Insert the correct forms of the adverbs (in parentheses) into these sentences:

1. My friend dances _____ than me. (gracefully)
2. She sings _____ as well. (beautifully)
3. She participated in the dancing and singing contests _____ than all of us. (frequently)
4. I believe she will perform at the next concert _____. (successfully)
5. My friend also studies English the _____ in class. (hard)
6. She always behaves _____. (respectfully)
7. Like a star she shines the _____ of all. (bright)

76

Choose the correct forms of the adjectives and adverbs (in parentheses) and insert them into these contexts:

1. (good, better, best, well)
   Have a _____ dream. Dream _____!
   I dream to speak _____ English.
   Now I understand English speakers a lot _____.
   I want to become the _____ English student in the world.
   How will I become at least the _____ in class?
2. (late, later, latest)
   He came _____ tonight.
   Yeah, he took the _____ bus.
   Why? I don't know. Anyway I'll speak to him _____.
3. (beautiful, more beautiful, most beautifully)
   I got a _____ birthday gift today. Really?
   Yes, my husband gave me a _____ gift this year than last year.
   But _____, he didn't forget my birthday this year.

Use the adjectives and adverbs from the box to complete the text below. Change their forms wherever necessary:

Interesting, fast, slow, well, careful, many, glad, active, exciting, happy

Our English teacher told us an _____ story today. Usually she speaks _____ but today she spoke much _____ for us to understand it _____. We listened to her story very _____. Then we asked her _____ questions and she _____ answered them all. We participated in this class more _____ than before. The teacher promised to tell _____ stories again to make us _____.

Answer the following questions about the general things and your personal situations:

1. Who sings most beautifully in the world?
2. Which star shines most brightly/the brightest in the clear night sky?
3. What animal moves most slowly/the slowest?
4. When do you need to walk the fastest?
5. Who drives most carefully in your family?
6. Who lives closest to your home?
7. Whom do you love most dearly?

5. Text

Speak about your future. Use the following questions to guide you:

1. How often do you think or worry about your future?
2. What goal do you have for the near future?
3. How long will you need to work on achieving your goal?
4. What did you do last month toward your goal?
5. What next goal will you set after you achieve this one?

Write down your goals:

1. To learn new skills...
2.
3.

Speak about your usual activities. Use these phrases:
Every day… On weekends… All the time… Monthly... Once a year...

Speak about your past activities. Mention what you did:
Yesterday… The day before yesterday… Three days ago… Last week...

Speak about your possible future activities. Use these ideas:
Sooner than later… Tonight… The day after tomorrow… In a day…

Make stories:

1. Talk about what you did in the past that you still do at present and you think you will do in the future.
2. Share your goals or dreams. Mention how you plan to fulfill them, and what you do toward them now.
3. Speak about the most memorable event in your life. Explain why you remember it and how it influences your present and how it will possibly change your future life.

Homework:
1. Watch the "Sounds American" videos about the flap /t̬/, glottal stop /ʔ/, and the dark /ɫ/.
2. Look up more information about the Future Simple tense.

Lesson 7

Text: **About me**

Affirmatives, negatives, and questions with the **present** forms of the verb '**be**':

- I **am**…/I am doing…
- She/He/It **is**…/She/He/It is doing…
- You/We/They **are**…/You/We/They are doing…

Tag questions: You're a student, aren't you?

Verbs: the Present Progressive tense/Present passive voice

Present participle: verb + **ing**: asking, doing, going, writing, greeting

Past participle: verb + **ed**: asked, greeted

Future forms: do/will do/will be doing/be doing/be going to do

Pronouns: **possessive/reflexive**: mine, my own, myself

Pronunciation: contractions, reductions

1. Text

"About me"

What's up? How're you doing? It's time to introduce myself. You already met my family. This time I will be talking more about me, my, mine, myself, and my own. But don't worry you will have the chance to speak about you, your, yours, yourself, and your own too.

Here I am, a smiling guy! My name is Al. It's my nickname. I'm in my mid-forties. I live in the US. I'm a computer programmer. I am currently working at a software company. Last year I worked for an advertising agency. I studied a lot and upgraded my technical skills, so I updated my resume and got a more interesting job. I'm thinking of starting my own business one day. I'm also interested in history. I want to learn more about some historical events.

I'm married as I already mentioned. My wife is a stay-at-home mom, but she will resume her work as soon as our sons grow up. She is a nurse and she likes her occupation. She's also good at visual arts. She is an artist. She paints fine pictures. Our sons are still young. Our older son is 7 years old. He's an elementary school child. Our younger one* is a toddler. They are nice children. They are interested in toys. Of course! My family is happy when we're together. That's my story. What's yours? I'm sorry for talking so much about myself. Now tell me about yourself. I'm sure you're an interesting and accomplished person.

Highlight the following words, phrasal verbs, and phrases in the story and read these comments:

1. be in mid-forties (44-46), in one's early or late twenties/thirties/forties…
2. upgrade (improve, make better) — update (give the latest information)
3. a resume /ˈrɛzəˌmeɪ/ — to resume /rəˈzum/ (start again)
4. be interested **in**…
5. grow up (growing, grew, grown) = become a grown-up
6. be good **at**…
7. a toddler (1-3 years old), a baby, a preschooler, a teenager, an adult...
8. *one (impersonal pronoun) = a person/thing (of the same kind or already mentioned); plural: ones (loved ones); possessive form: one's (one's life).
9. accomplish = achieve, attain

2. Sentence

Affirmatives with the present tense verb **be**:
- I **am**…/am doing…
- She/He/It **is**…/is doing...
- You/We/They **are**…/are doing…

Negatives:
- I **am not**…/am not doing…
- She/He/It **is not** (**isn't**)…/is not doing...
- You/We/They **are not** (**aren't**)…/are not doing…

Yes/No questions:
- **Am** I…?/Am I doing…?
- **Is** she/he/it…?/Is she/he/it doing…?
- **Are** you/we/they…?/Are you/we/they doing…?

Wh-questions:
- Who **am** I?/What am I doing…?
- What **is** she/he/it doing…?
- What **are** you/we/they doing…?

Tag questions:
- I **am**…,/am doing…, **am I not**?
- I **am not**…,/am not doing…, **am I**?
- She/He/It **is**…,/is doing..., **isn't** she/he/it?
- She/He/It **is not**…,/is not doing..., **is** she/he/it?
- You/We/They **are**…,/are doing…, **aren't** you/we/they?
- You/We/They **are not**…,/are not doing…, **are** you/we/they?

In the story "About me" on page 79, locate the sentences that present different people. Begin:

1. I am (I'm) _____
2. You are (you're)_____
3. She is (she's) _____
4. He is (he's) _____
5. They are (they're) _____
6. We are (we're) _____

Information: **I'm**... **you're**... **she's**... are contractions (short forms) for easier and quicker speech in spoken English.

How to pronounce **affirmative** contractions with the verb **be**?

- I am /aɪəm/ → I'm /aɪm/
- You are /juɑr/ → You're /jɚ/
- She is /ʃɪɪz/ → She's /ʃiz/
- He is /hiɪz/ → He's /hiz/
- It is /ɪt̬ɪz/ → It's /ɪts/
- We are /wiɑr/ → We're /wɪr/
- They are /ðeɪɑr/ → They're /ðɚ/

What information do you get from the following statements? Match the answers to the possible questions in the right column:

Answers	Questions
1. I'm in my mid-forties.	A. How old are you?
2. I'm a computer programmer.	B. Are you married or single?
3. I am currently working at a software company.	C. What do you do?
4. I'm thinking of starting my own business one day.	D. Where do you work?
5. I'm interested in history.	E. Where do you live?
6. I'm married.	F. What are your interests?
7. I live in the US.	G. What is your dream?

Write down the questions if you want to ask someone about their:

- Name: _____
- Age: _____
- Occupation: _____
- Family status: _____
- Interests: _____
- Dreams: _____

<table>
<tr><td>

Active voice vs. passive voice

Active voice. The verb '**be**' is watching what's going on right now, what we're doing, and what we're going to do as well as what we do, did, and will do...
Passive voice. The verb '**be**' passively notices what is done to us or what is not done by us. Check it out.

</td></tr>
</table>

Identify when the verb 'be' **helps with the** <u>active voice</u> **and when the verb** 'be' **helps with the** <u>passive voice</u>. **Highlight and compare the verb forms**:

1. I am currently working at a software company.
2. I am currently employed by a software company.
3. My wife is painting now.
4. My wife's paintings are being shown at the art gallery these days.
5. We are raising two sons. They're growing up fast.
6. Our sons are raised by us.
7. My older son is riding on the school bus right now.
8. My older son is taken to school by a school bus.

Look at the pictures and read the descriptions of what people are <u>actively</u> **doing at the present moment**:

She's smiling.   They're laughing.   He's running.   I'm feeling happy.   We're working.

Compare the verb forms that describe the actions, which happen usually, and the actions, which are happening now (in progress now):

1. I **exercise** every day. I **am exercising** right now.
2. He normally **drives** to his work. He **is driving** to his work at this moment.
3. She **paints** in her free time. She **is painting** in her studio now.
4. We regularly **study** English. We **are studying** English now.
5. They **eat** vegetables all the time. They **are eating** vegetables right now.

Present time ➔ the Present Progressive tense ➔ continuous actions

How to form the **Present Progressive tense**?

➔ the **helping** verb 'be' + present participle of the **main** verb

The verb '**be**' changes: I **am**...

You **are**…
She/He/It (also singular nouns) **is**…
We **are**...
They (also plural nouns) **are**...

Present participle: verb + **ing**

begin ➔ begi**nn**ing
buy ➔ buying
come ➔ coming
get ➔ ge**tt**ing
give ➔ giving
go ➔ going
visit ➔ visiting

Example: I **am watering** my plants right now.

Imagine that these regular activities are actually happening now. Change the verb tense and the adverbs of time. Rewrite these sentences:

1. My parents **visit** me every weekend. _____.
2. We **shop** for groceries once a week. _____.
3. My English teacher often **tells** us funny stories. _____.
4. My pet **sleeps** all the time. _____.
5. We sometimes **watch** the sunset. _____.

What are you/they not doing when you/they are doing something else? Complete the sentences below. Use the verbs in parentheses if necessary:

For example: My students aren't talking when they're listening to my stories.

1. When I _____ (learn English), I _____ (watch television).
2. They _____ (listen to loud music) when they _____ (work).
3. We _____ (talk) when we _____ (eat).
4. My parents _____ (walk) when it _____ (rain).
5. My sister _____ (drive) when it _____ (snow).
6. The kids _____ (eat) when they _____ (play).
7. My friend _____ (check emails) when she _____ (study).

How to pronounce **negative** contractions with the verb **be**?

- I am not → I'm not
- You are not → You aren't /'arənt/
- She is not → She isn't /'ıznt/
- He is not → He isn't
- It is not → It isn't /ıt'ıznt/
- We are not → We aren't
- They are not → They aren't
- I/You/She/He/It/We/They → ain't /eınt/ (very informal)

Identify the types of the questions in the following conversation. Choose one of these types and write them down:
1. Yes/No question
2. Wh-question
3. Tag question

- It's a pretty day, isn't it /'ıznıt/ (first "t" is silent)? Yes, it is. _____
- Where are you heading? We're going to the park. _____
- You don't walk there, do you? No, we don't. It's a long walk. _____
- How're you getting there? By bus. _____
- You like that park, don't you? Yes, we do. Very much! _____
- Are you enjoying your time there? Yes, we are. _____
- Who wants to stay in on such a beautiful day? (rhetorical question)
  _____

How to ask **tag** questions?

Affirmative statement, **negative** tag?
Negative statement, **affirmative** tag?

1. You **like** your ↘job, **don't** ↗you? ↘Yes, I ↘do./↘No, I ↘don't.
2. I **am making** ↘lunch, am I ↗not? ↘Yes, you ↘are./↗↘No, you ↘aren't.
3. They're ↘coming over, ↗**aren't** they? I'm ↘not sure.
4. She ↘**doesn't live** here, ↗**does** she? Yes, she does. (She lives here.)/No, she doesn't. (She doesn't live here.)
5. He **is** her ↘brother, ↗**isn't he** /ˈɪzni/ ("t"/"h" are silent)? Yes, he is./No, he isn't.
6. You **will teach** me, **won't** you? Yes, I will./No, I won't.
7. We didn't interrupt your conversation, **did** we? Yes, you did./No, you didn't.

Add the question tags to these sentences:

- You will help me with this task tomorrow, _____?
- You are helping me with the task tomorrow, _____?
- You help me with the task tomorrow, _____?
- You aren't going to help me with the task tomorrow, _____?

Notice: All the sentences in the above exercise refer to the future:

1. Will you help me tomorrow? Yes, I will.
2. Are you helping me tomorrow? Yes, I am.
3. Do you help me tomorrow? Yes, I do.
4. Are you going to help me tomorrow? Yes, I'm.

Four principal ways of referring to the future:

1. I hope I **will travel** when I retire./I hope **I'll be traveling** a lot when I retire. (Future Simple/Future Progressive)
2. I made plans. I **am going to travel** to Europe next month. (be going to…)
3. You know. I **am traveling** to Europe next month. (Present Progressive)
4. I need to get to the airport. I **travel** in two hours. (Present Simple)

   (**Note**: It's not a mistake to use all the future forms interchangeably.)

Passive voice. Sometimes we are not the subjects of our actions. Something or someone else is at the forefront of the actions.

Compare the sentences in active voice and passive voice:

1. My sister **is helping** me around my house now. I **am being helped by** my sister with my household chores right now.
2. My sister often **cooks**, so our meals **are** often **cooked by** my sister. But I'm a good cook, too. Next time our meals **will be prepared by** me. They **won't be made by** my sister. However, I always praise the food prepared by my sister and my cooking **is** always **praised by** my sister.
3. I **do** the laundry, so the laundry **is done by** me. I also **vacuum** the carpet, so the carpet **is vacuumed by** me.
4. My sister **sweeps and mops** the floors, so the floors **are swept and mopped by** my sister. She also **waters** the plants, so the plants **are watered** by my sister, therefore they grow so happily.

Active voice (present): My sister **helps** me all the time.
> She **is helping** me now. ➜ be + Present Participle

Passive voice (present): I'm **helped by** my sister. ➜ be + Past Participle
> I **am being helped** by her now. ➜ be + being + Past Participle

Present Participle		Past Participle	
Verb + ing		Regular verb + ed	Irregular verbs
agreeing	beginning	agreed	begun
competing	breaking	completed	broken
introducing	bringing	introduced	brought
identifying	choosing	identified	chosen
playing	showing	played	shown
traveling	putting	traveled	put
washing	eating	washed	eaten
watching…	falling	watched…	fallen
	giving		given
	keeping		kept
	knowing		known
	writing…		written…

So the verb **be** is another important verb in English. It helps with many things:

1. It helps identify people and things.
   For example: I **am** an English student. You **are** an English teacher. It**'s** an English book.
2. It helps describe continuous actions (actions in progress).
   (Maybe, that's why the Present Progressive tense form is longer than the Present Simple tense, which mostly states facts and describes routines. Just a thought.)
   Compare: I **am studying** English. (I study English.) She **is teaching** English. (She teaches English.) We **are reading** an English book. (We read books.)
3. It also helps form the passive voice.
   For example: English **is being studied** by me. English **is taught** by her. An English book **is read** by us.
   (But it's often better to communicate ideas in the active voice unless we want to make someone or something else more important than ourselves. Speaking of ourselves…)

3. Words

Pronouns:
- possessive
- reflexive

1. What is a pronoun? Pronoun = pro + noun, so a pronoun is like a noun.
2. What pronouns do we know?
   - personal pronouns: I, you, she, he, it, we, they
   - impersonal pronouns: one/no one, someone, anyone, everyone…
   - possessive pronouns: my, your, her, his, its, our, their

(**Note**: possessive nouns: my teacher**'s** book → teacher + **'s**; Mother**'s** Day; my son's friend; **but** our teacher<u>s</u>' books; customers' reviews)

3. What other pronouns does English have? Let's find out.

What do the pronouns 'my own' 'yours' and 'myself'/'yourself' mean in the story "About me" on page 79?

- I'm thinking of starting **my own** business one day.
- That's my story. What's **yours**?
- I'm sorry for talking so much about **myself**. Now tell me about **yourself**.

Information: the pronoun '**own**' /oʊn/ means belonging to someone;
the noun '**self**' means one's essence; and
the pronoun '**one'self**' refers to a speaker herself/himself...

Find the categories of the above-mentioned pronouns in this chart:

Subject	Object	Possessive (before nouns)	Possessive (without nouns)	Possessive (with 'own')	Reflexive (with 'self')
I	me	my	mine	my own	myself
You	you	your	yours	your own	yourself
She	her	her	hers	her own	herself
He	him	his	his	his own	himself
It	it	its	its	its own	itself
You	you	your	yours	your own	yourselves
We	us	our	ours	our own	ourselves
They	them	their	theirs	their own	themselves

Distinguish between the <u>possessive</u> and <u>reflexive</u> pronouns in the contexts below. Underscore the possessive and circle the reflexive pronouns:

1. I live in my own house. My house is small but it is mine. I built it myself and I live by myself.
2. My parents live on their own. They prefer to live by themselves. I respect their decision. The choice is theirs.
3. You're driving a big car. Is it yours?
   Yes, it is.
   Do you fix your car yourself if it gets any problems?
   I change oil myself but it's not easy to fix serious problems on one's own, so I take my car to a mechanic in case it has a big issue.
4. Whatever we own is ours, isn't it?
   Yes, whatever we bought ourselves.
   So this tree in our yard isn't ours because you didn't buy it.
   It's not ours but we will enjoy it for some time.

5. Whose painting is this?

   It's mine.

   Do you mean you painted it yourself?

   No, I just own it. It's my own possession.

Familiarize yourself with these words and phrases:

- build (building–built–built) = construct
- by myself/on their own = independently
- fix one's car/problem = repair one's car/solve one's problem
- serious = important
- own (owning–owned–owned) = have, possess
- whatever = anything, any kind
- possession/possessions = something owned

Insert the proper pronouns in the following conversations:

1. Are these _____ eyeglasses?

   No, they aren't _____.

2. Did anyone help you with this serious task?

   No, I finished it _____.

3. Are you hungry?

   Yes, I'm.

   Then help _____ in the kitchen.

4. You're always busy, aren't you?

   Yes, I'm.

   It's because you do everything _____.

5. If we buy our _____ house, we'll live on our _____.

   You're right. We will live by _____ then.

6. They think of _____ as important people.

   Don't we think of _____ in the same way?

7. I saw my new neighbor and introduced _____.

   Awesome! What did you say about _____?

8. They have a big garden.

   Is _____ garden much bigger than _____?

   I think so. But _____ garden is nicer than _____.

9. Hi. Are you new here?

   Yes, I am.

   What's _____ name?

   I'm Steve. What's _____?

4. Sentence

Read this humorous talk between a kitten and a bird. Act it out with your friend or classmate:

> Where are you going, little kitten?
>> I am going to school, birdie.
>
> Will I fly with you, little cat?
>> Yes, you're welcome, dear birdie. But what are you going to do in school?
>
> What do you do in school, little kitten?
>> I learn to read and count there.
>> Then I will study letters and numbers too.
>> But you won't sit long at the desk. You will soon fly away.
>
> Okay then. What are you doing after school, dear kitten?
>> I'm going to the library after school.
>
> Why are you going to the library, little kitten?
>> Because knowledge is my fortune, dear birdie.
>
> Mine, too. Will I join you in the library, little kitten?
>> Oh no. You're gonna* fly around and make noise, dear birdie.
>
> Okay then. I don't wanna* make noise. Bye, little kitten. Study well and learn to fly too. Then we're gonna be friends and fly together. See you, little kitten.

*The words '**gonna**' and '**wanna**' are called reductions (reduced forms). They're used in very informal spoken English: gonna = going to; wanna = want to. Also: gimme = give me; lemme = let me, gotcha = got ya (you), etc. Just FYI (for your information), not to be used yet.

Fill in the blanks with the missing words in this phone conversation. Some verbs are given in parentheses:

- Hi! Are _____ busy right now?
- No, I'm not. I'm _____ doing anything special right now. Why _____ you asking?
- Well. I'm _____ (have) a guest right now. We _____ planning to eat out. _____ you in the mood for Italian food?
- Yes, I _____. I enjoy pasta. Are _____ going out soon?
- Not right _____ but in an hour. Are you _____ (join) us?

- Sure. Which restaurant are we _____(go) to?
- Near me. In my neighborhood.
- Great! I'm _____(come) over there?
- How are you _____ (get) here?
- I'm _____ (get) a car service.
- Wonderful! See you in a bit.

You're a new person at a company. You're asked many questions. Here they are. What are your answers?

1. How are* you* doing?_____
2. Is it your first day on the job?_____
3. Are you a new engineer here?_____
4. Are you only working or are you also studying?_____
5. What are you doing right now?_____
6. Which office are you sitting in?_____
7. You're okay with this desk, aren't you?_____

(*the word '**are**' is sometimes omitted and '**you**' is reduced to '**ya**' or '**yuh**' in informal, friendly "greetings": How ya doing?)

Describe what people are doing in these pictures:

_____   _____   _____   _____   _____

Define things, occupations, and concepts. Finish the sentences below.
For example: "*Knowledge is power.*" (Francis Bacon)
　　　　　"*Philosophy is doubt.*" (Montaigne)

An apple is a fruit.
A book is _____
A student is _____
A teacher is _____
History is _____
Ignorance is _____

5. Text

Introduce yourself. Mention:

- Your name: _____
- Your occupation: _____
- Your age (optional): _____
- Your marital status (optional): _____
- Your interests: _____
- Your plans and dreams: _____

Write a story about yourself:

Hi! My name's…

Share your future activities. Use these questions to prompt you:

1. What do you hope you will do in the near future?
2. What are you going to do soon for sure?
3. What are you doing tomorrow?
4. What do you do next weekend?

Your friend is texting you and asking what you're doing. Text her/him/them back answering her/his/their question in great detail. Write your long text here:

_____

_____

_____

Homework:
Look up information about the Present Progressive tense and Present passive voice online.

Lesson 8

Text: **There I was...**

Affirmatives, negatives, and questions with the **past** forms of the verb '**be**':
- I/She/He/It **was**.../I/She/He/It was doing...
- You/We/They **were**.../You/We/They were doing...

Verbs: the Past Progressive tense/Past passive voice
Storytelling elements: characters, setting, plot, idea, theme
Indirect speech: that, whether, wh-words
Pronunciation: linking

---

1. Text

Now you're ready for more interesting reads, aren't you? You're going to read a short story based on Mark Twain's story "The Million Pound Bank Note." Mark Twain (1835-1910) was an American writer. He is known for his novels about the adventures of Tom Sawyer and Huckleberry Finn.

The title of this story is "**There I was...**"

There I was in London, hungry and hopeless. I was dragging myself along some wealthy place. I was starving. It was a cold, rainy morning. How did I end up so  far away from my home?

I was a clerk in San Francisco. I was 27 years old. I was a free man although alone in the world. I was intelligent and respected. My time was my own after work. I used to sail on my boat. One day I was sailing too far and I was carried out to sea. At night, when I lost hope, I was picked up by a small ship, which was heading for London. It was a long and stormy voyage. I worked as a sailor without pay. When I arrived in London, my clothes were shabby and my pocket was empty.

So I was desperately dragging myself along the street when I heard, "Step in, please." It was a servant. He led me into the grand room where two elderly gentlemen were sitting. They were having their lavish breakfast. I was losing my mind at seeing the food but I wasn't offered to sample it. They didn't tell me why they wanted to see me. They just gave me an envelope with a one million pound banknote.

I immediately went to a cheap restaurant. After I ate, I gave the banknote to pay and asked for change. Upon seeing the banknote, the restaurant owner told me not to worry about paying. Then I decided to buy myself new clothes. The same happened at a store. The store manager gave me clothes on credit. Soon I became a celebrity. I was invited to dinner parties. My celebrity was used by some company to endorse their products and I received commission. Once at a party, I met a young woman. I told her my story and she found it funny. At the end of the month, we went to see the elderly gentlemen who were actually brothers. One brother was the young woman's stepfather. They made a bet and he won it and out of joy he asked me to become his son-in-law. The bet was that I would return the banknote unspent because simply showing the possession of money was enough to survive and even get rich.

Familiarize yourself with the following words, phrases, and phrasal verbs. Highlight them in the story:

1. drag oneself = walking, moving, or pulling slowly with efforts
2. end up = come to a situation that is not planned
3. head for = move toward
4. arrive at = reach a destination, result, or solution
5. desperately = helplessly
6. lose one's mind = become confused or crazy
7. sample food = taste food
8. ask for change = ask for the money as the balance of the amount paid
9. endorse = recommend
10. bet = a risk of money due to an agreement
11. unspent = without spending
12. survive = live on

Take note of these similar phrases that have different meanings:

- I **used** + **to do** something. = I did something repeatedly only in the <u>past</u>.
- I **am/was used by** someone. = I provide/provided a service to someone.
- I **am/was used** + **to doing** something. = I have/had a <u>habit</u> of doing something.

From the list below, choose the words that relate to:

Sea: _____

Money: _____

> Banknote, voyage, bet, sail, change, ship, commission, credit, boat, rich, sailor, pay, expensive, cheap, possession

2. Sentence

Affirmatives with the past forms of the verb **be**:
- I/She/He/It **was**…/was doing…
- You/We/They **were**…/ were doing…

Negatives:
- I/She/He/It **wasn't** (was not)…/wasn't (was not) doing…
- You/We/They **weren't** (were not)…/were not (weren't) doing…

Yes/No questions:
- **Was** I/she/he/it…?/Was I/she/he/it doing…?
- **Were** you/we/they…?/Were you/we/they doing…?

Wh-questions:
- What **was** I/she/he/it doing…?
- What **were** you/we/they doing…?

Tag questions:
- I/She/He/It **was**…,/was doing, **wasn't** I/she/he/it?
- I/She/He/It **was not** (**wasn't**)…,/was not doing..., **was** I/she/he/it?
- You/We/They **were**…,/were doing…, **weren't** you/we/they?
- You/We/They **were not** (**weren't**)…,/were not doing…, **were** you/we/they?

Highlight the past tense of the verb 'be' **in these sentences**:

1. It was a long and stormy voyage.
2. It was a cold rainy morning. I was starving.
3. I was dragging myself along some wealthy place.
4. Two elderly gentlemen were sitting in the room.
5. They were having their lavish breakfast.
6. I was not invited to eat.

Compare the verb forms that refer to the present and past actions:

- I **am** in London. I **was** in London.
- I **am starving**. I **was starving**.
- It **is** a cold morning. It **was** a cold morning.
- They **are having** breakfast. They **were having** breakfast when I saw them.
- I'm **invited** to parties. I **was invited** to parties.

Past time ➔ the Past Progressive tense ➔ continuous actions in the past

The **Past Progressive** tense is formed:
- I/She/He/It **was/wasn't** + verb-**ing** (present participle)... ➔ I was starving.
- You/We/They **were/weren't** + verb-**ing** (present participle)... ➔ They were eating.

The **Past Passive voice** is formed:
- I/She/He/It **was/wasn't** + verb-**ed** (past participle)... ➔ I was invited to eat.
- You/We/They **were/weren't** + verb-**ed** (past participle)... ➔ They weren't invited to eat.

Change the present tense of the verb 'be' to its past tense and rewrite the sentences:

1. I'm watching TV. _____
2. I'm served dinner. _____
3. We are having a birthday party. _____
4. We're happy. _____
5. We are giving love. _____
6. We are given love. _____

The **Past Progressive tense** is **used** to describe an action in progress at a certain time in the past.

- My dad **was cooking when I came home**. He was hungry because he was working in the garden **all morning**. My mom **was helping** him **while my dad was cooking**. She was setting the table. She was putting plates, forks, and spoons on the dining table.
- They were working on an important project **all day yesterday**. I joined them **when** they were finishing it. But still they were thankful to me.

The **Past Passive voice** is used to emphasize the effect of some past actions on someone or something.

- I **was not invited** to sample food. I wasn't even offered to have a seat.
- The story **was written** by me. It was published last year.

Observe the use of the Past Progressive tense:

- I lost my phone. I was desperately looking for it **when** it rang. Someone was calling me at that moment and it helped me recover the phone. I was lucky. It was actually my mom who called me.
- My mom asked me what I **was doing at the moment**. I told her that I was looking for my phone when she called. Then she broke the news. Her friend from Florida was going to visit her.

Compare continuing actions in the past as opposed to completed actions in the past:

- I **slept** badly last night. When I **was sleeping**, I heard a loud knock at the door. It was a delivery. They delivered my order while I was still sleeping. It wasn't very early. I was just sleeping till late morning.
- I finally decided to move to New York. I was deciding all year. I was weighing the pros and cons before I decided to move to NY.

Answer the questions in relation to the above-described situations:

1. What was your dad doing when you came home? Why was he cooking? What was your mom doing while your dad was cooking?
2. Why were you looking for your phone? Who was calling you when you were looking for your phone? What did your mom tell you when she called you? Who was coming to visit your mom?
3. How did you sleep last night? What were you doing when you heard a loud knock at the door? What was happening while you were sleeping? Why were you sleeping so late? Were you sick?

Write down the answers to the questions about the story "There I was…":

- What happened to the man one day when he was sailing too far? _____
  _____
- Why was the man starving? _____
- What happened when he was dragging himself? _____
  _____
- What were two gentlemen doing when he saw them? _____
  _____
- What breakfast were they eating? _____

3. Words

Storytelling elements:
- character(s), setting, plot
- idea, theme

Pair the following concepts to their definitions:

Concepts	Definitions
What is a **story**? What is an **event**? Who's a **character**? What is a **setting**? What's a **plot**? What is an **idea**? What is a **theme**?	• It is usually a description of the characters' experiences and behaviors in the circumstances of real or imaginary events. It's a narrative. • It is a person in a story who is a storyteller himself/herself or someone whom a story is narrated about. • It is an incident or an extraordinary happening. • It is a description of the time and place to give the mood for a story. It sometimes includes a historical, social, or personal background. • It is a message, moral, or a lesson to be taken away from a story. • It is a reason why a story is told and shared with others. • It is a storyline with the introduction of a problem (exposition), rising of a conflict, peak of emotional tension (climax), resolution, and/or ending (outcome).

Before we move on to the discussion of the story "**There I was...**," it's good to learn about and practice an important aspect of pronunciation called **linking /‿/**. Linking is connecting words to make them sound together. In English, words are not separated. They are smoothly linked.

Read the following definitions of the story elements and link the words.
The linking symbols are shown for the first three numbers.
For example: A⌣character is⌣a⌣person in⌣a⌣story. **Fill in the symbols /⌣/**
in the other sentences:

1. What⌣is⌣an⌣event? It⌣is⌣an⌣incident.
2. What⌣is⌣a⌣setting? A⌣setting⌣is a⌣description of⌣the⌣time⌣and place.
3. An⌣idea⌣is a⌣reason behind⌣an⌣event.
4. What is a plot? It is a storyline.
5. A story is a narrative.
6. A theme is the main takeaway from a story.
7. What is a conflict in a story? It's a character's external and/or internal struggle.

What do you know about the character's background in the story "There I was…" on page 93? Write down the known information about the character:

Age: He was twenty-seven years old.
Job: _____
Hometown: _____
Family status: _____
Interests: _____
Qualities: _____

What is the story's setting? Find the description of the time and place in the story. Write your associations with the place and time mentioned in the story:

- London: It's the capital of Great Britain. I was in London. I liked the city.
- San Francisco: _____
- a cold, rainy morning: _____

Connect the words in the sentences that define the concepts of place and time with the missing function words:

- **Place** ___ ___ particular point ___space; it ___ ___ area occupied and used ___ someone.
- **Time** ___ ___ existence measured ___ epochs, periods, centuries, ages, decades, years, months, days, hours, minutes, ____ seconds.

Describe the place of your residence. Mention the continent, country, and the city or town where you live. Use the help of the questions and the table below. Include the name of your country and its capital into the table if that information is missing:

1. What country do you live in? _____
2. What is the capital of your country? _____
3. Which continent does your country belong to? _____
4. Where is your hometown located in the country? _____
5. How many people live in your hometown? _____
6. What is your country and hometown known for? _____
7. What do you like about your place? _____

_____

Continents	Countries	Capitals
Africa	Argentina	Buenos Aires
Antarctica	Algeria	Algiers
Asia	Australia	Canberra
Australia	Brazil	Brasilia
Europe	Canada	Ottawa
North America	China	Beijing
South America	India	New Delhi
	Kazakhstan	Nur-Sultan
	Russia	Moscow
	United States of America	Washington D.C.
	_____	_____

Describe the time of your existence. Mention the century, year, season, month, day, hour, minutes, and seconds of your present lifetime. Use the questions and the information in the box below for your reference:

1. What century do you live in? _____
2. What year is it now? _____
3. What month of the year is now? _____
4. What season is it now in your country? _____
5. What is the weather like in this season? _____
6. What date is it today? _____
7. What time is it now? _____

Century: the eighteenth, nineteenth, twentieth, twenty-first century

Year: the year 1995 (nineteen ninety five), 2000 (two thousand), 2020 (twenty twenty), 2021 (twenty twenty one or two thousand twenty one), 2030 (twenty thirty)

Seasons: winter, spring, summer, fall (autumn)

Weather: cold, warm, hot, cool, rainy, snowy, sunny, cloudy, partly cloudy, partly sunny, clear sky, thunderstorms, 45 degrees Fahrenheit, 10 degrees Celsius

Months: January, February /ˈfɛbjuˌ(w)ɛri/ (the first letter "r" is silent), March, April, May, June, July, August, September, October, November, December

Date: It's Friday, January 1st, 2021; Tuesday, February 23rd; Monday, March 2nd; Saturday, April 12th; a week starts on Sunday; a week is Sunday through Saturday

Time: It's 9:30 (nine thirty/half past nine), 8:15 (a quarter past eight); 11:45 (a quarter to twelve); 12:20 (twenty past twelve); 3:50 (ten to four)

Parts of the day: 12 pm/noon; 12 am/midnight; from 12 am to 12 pm: 1 o'clock in the morning, 4 am; 1 pm/1 o'clock in the afternoon; 5 pm/5 o'clock in the evening

If you have access to Alexa, ask her these questions. Write down her answers:

- Alexa, what century is it now? _____
- Alexa, what day of the week is it today? _____
- Alexa, how's the weather today? _____
- Alexa, what's the time now? _____
- Alexa, what should I wear today? _____

Imagine the details of the setting in the story "There I was…":

1. What season of the year was it if "it was a cold, rainy morning"?

   _____

2. What is the weather like in London? _____

3. What is the weather like in San Francisco? _____
4. Who was the story "The Million Pound Bank Note" written by? _____
5. What century was it if the story was published in 1893? _____

What is the plot of the story? **Give a plot summary. Continue writing**:

Exposition. The main character from San Francisco turned up in London, hungry and hopeless. _____
_____

Conflict. He was given an envelope with the million pound banknote.
_____
_____

Climax. He went to a cheap restaurant. _____
_____

Resolution. He became a celebrity. _____
_____

Ending. He was going to become a son-in-law. _____
_____

Find the clues (information) in the story about the main idea and theme. Pick an option from the choices below or give your own answer:

1. What is the story "There I was…" about? It is about:
    a. the man who ended up in London
    b. the man who survived his life's disaster and even made a fortune
    c. the situation that helped the man overcome his hardship
    d. the event that changed the man's destiny
    e. _____

2. What message did you take away from the story?
    a. "There is only one class that thinks more about money than the rich, and that is the poor." (Oscar Wilde)
    b. It's good to be at the right place at the right time.
    c. It's enough to show money to be respected.
    d. "Make money and the whole world will conspire to call you a gentleman." (Mark Twain)
    e. _____

Letters ➔ words:

Make short stories with the last letters of the alphabet. For example:

Once the letter "A" was a red apple. But I ate it. It was a very tasty apple!
Once the letter "B" was a book. And I read it. Then I knew it was a good book!

- Once the letter "**T**" was _____
- Once the letter "**U**" was _____
- Once the letter "**V**" was _____
- Once the letter "**W**" was _____
- Once the letter "**X**" was _____
- Once the letter "**Y**" was _____
- Once the letter "**Z**" was _____

4. Sentence

Read one of the wise fables by Aesop:

"The Travelers and the Tree"

It was a hot summer day. At noon, two Travelers lay down* under the wide branches of a Tree. While they were resting under its shade, one traveler said to the other, "This tree is useless."
The other one agreed, "It gives no fruits to satisfy our hunger."
The Tree interrupted them and said, "You're so ungrateful!" Then it asked:
"Are you describing me as useless while resting under my shade?"

(*lay down = past tense of 'lie down')

In the above Aesop's story, gather the information about:

- the setting: _____
- the characters: _____
- the plot: _____
- the idea: _____
- the moral: _____

In the fable, change the direct speech into indirect speech. Use the sentences provided below the table. First, familiarize yourself with the explanation of how to change direct speech into indirect one:

Direct and indirect speech

Direct speech: I asked myself: "Why do I spend so much time on social media?"
Indirect speech: I asked myself why I spent so much time on social media."

Direct speech	Indirect speech
1. A servant said, "**Step** in, please." 2. Our teacher asked us, "Please **don't** be late for the classes." 3. She **says** to her neighbor, "You**'re** such a compassionate person. Thank you for your generous help." 4. My boss **asked** me, "**Are** you free to discuss a new project now?" 5. He **asked**, "What do you **plan** to do **tomorrow**?" 6. They **said**, "We are leaving **now**."	1. A servant asked **to step** in. 2. Our teacher asked us **not** to be late for the classes. 3. She **says** to her neighbor **that** her neighbor **is** such a compassionate person. She thanks her/him for her/his generous help. 4. My boss **asked** me **whether I was** free to discuss a new project **at that time**. 5. He **asked** what I **planned** to do the **next day**. 6. They **said** that they **were** leaving **at that time**.

- One traveler said to the other, "This tree is useless." → _____
  _____

- The other one agreed, "It gives no fruits to satisfy our hunger." → _____

- The tree interrupted them and said, "You're so ungrateful!" → _____

- It asked: "Are you describing me as useless while resting under my shade?" →
  _____

Compare your answers to these ones. Highlight the changes made in the indirect speech:

- One traveller said to the other that the tree was useless.

- The other one agreed that it gave no fruits to satisfy their hunger.
- The tree interrupted them and said that they were so ungrateful.
- It asked whether they were describing it as useless while resting under its shade.

How to **report** someone's speech?

1. Use the following conjunctions: **that/which**, **whether/if**, **wh-words**
   Statements ➜ 'that' or no conjunction:
   A traveler said, "This tree is useless." ➜ A traveler said (that) the tree was useless.
   Yes/No questions ➜ 'whether' or 'if':
   The tree asked, "Are you describing me as useless while resting under my shade?" ➜ The tree asked whether they were describing it as useless while resting under its shade.
   Wh-questions ➜ wh-words:
   He asked me, "Why do you want to leave **now**?" ➜ He asked me why I wanted to leave **then**.
2. Change the tense and adverbs if they refer to the past
   My boss **asked** me, "What do I plan to do **tomorrow**?" ➜ My boss asked me what I **planned** to do **the next day**.
   But no change in case of the present tense: My mom always **asks** me, "Why don't you visit me more often?" ➜ My mom always asks me why I don't visit her more often.
3. Follow the usual statement word order: S + V (conjunction) S + V
   They asked a receptionist, "Where is the restroom **here**? ➜ They asked a receptionist where the restroom was **there**.
   I was asked, "Where are you?" ➜ I was asked where I was.

---

5. Text

Read an imaginary conversation between the man and two gentlemen based on the story "There I was…" on page 93. Report it back in the indirect speech:

- When the man saw two gentlemen, he surprisingly asked them, "Why do you want to see me, sirs?" _____
- After a pause, one of the gentlemen asked the man, "What do you do in London?" _____
- I told them my story: "I'm in London by accident…" _____
- The other gentleman commented: "That's an interesting story. _____

- Then he asked me, "What are you going to do now?" _____
  _____
- I replied, "I'm hungry and I'm looking for a shelter." _____
  _____
- After that, he handed me a letter and said: "Do not open it now. Read it outside and follow the written instructions." _____
  _____

Relate the story "There I was…" as a storyteller (from the third person). Use the following plan if necessary:

1. It was a cold rainy morning in London.
2. The man was hungry and penniless.
3. He was a clerk in San Francisco.
4. One day he was carried out to sea.
5. He ended up in London.
6. A servant led him into a room.
7. He was given an envelope by two gentlemen.
8. He went to a restaurant.
9. He became a celebrity.
10. He met a young woman.
11. It was a bet.

Remember an interesting event from your life and write a story about it with yourself as a character. Describe the setting, the conflict, and the resolution:

Title:
Setting:
Character(s):
Plot: **There I was**…

Thank you!

Homework:
Look up information about the Past Progressive tense, Past passive voice, and the rules of indirect speech.

Lesson 9

Text: **Here I have...**
The Present Perfect/Present Perfect Progressive/Past Perfect tense: '**have done/have been doing**.../**had done**...'
Description of things: **This** is/was.../**These** are/were... **There** is/are... was/were...
Prepositions and adverbs of **time**: for, since, before, recently, lately...
Prepositions and adverbs of **place**: in, out, indoors, outdoors, inside, outside...
Pronunciation: final stop consonants, vowels before voiced and voiceless consonants

---

1. Text

"Here I have..."

Here I have something that is very dear to me. It's a letter from my beloved mother. She had written the letter shortly before she left this plane. She wrote:

My dearest daughter,

We haven't seen each other for several months now but I feel as if it had been for a very long time. You asked me how I had been. I've been okay except that I miss you a lot. I've always been thinking about you since you left.
I want to tell you that I love you so much that my heart hurts. You have always been a beautiful sunray in my life. My life had been hard before you grew up and established yourself as a successful and intelligent person. My life is looking up now. I've been experiencing more joy and happiness in my life since then as you lovingly take care of me. I'm happy that you have accomplished a lot in your life. Please keep up the amazing work! At the same time, as you grow older, it's good to seek spiritual knowledge. As life passes by, you will inevitably ask yourself many meaningful questions that are not answered in conventional books. They are answered in sacred books. Such books have helped me tremendously. Thanks to them, I have attained peace and balance in my life and, most importantly—fearlessness. I know now that fear of losing worldly attachments comes from the lack of true knowledge. That's all I want to tell you for now, my love. It's a little wisdom that a person has acquired with time and, as a parent, wants to share with their children. Take care of yourself and your family. Thank you for your love. I love you too.
Your mom.

Find the following <u>adjectives</u> in the text. Change them to adverbs:

Beautiful – _____; successful – _____
Intelligent – _____; happy – _____; sacred – _____
Amazing – _____; spiritual – _____
Meaningful – _____; conventional – _____

Find the following <u>adverbs</u> in the text. Change them to adjectives:

Shortly – _____; inevitably – _____
Tremendously – _____; importantly – _____

Highlight the following verbs, phrasal verbs, and phrases in the text:

1. plane = existence
2. miss = feel sad at not seeing someone
3. establish oneself = prove oneself
4. look up (about life) = improve, become better
5. experience = feel, have
6. take care of = help, look after
7. seek = look for
8. worldly = material, earthly
9. lack = absence
10. acquire = get, learn

Among these nouns from the text, pick out and underline <u>abstract nouns</u>:

A letter, heart, life, a person, joy, happiness, care, work, knowledge, truth, a question, a book, an attachment, peace, balance, fearlessness, fear, wisdom, time, children, a family, love

Bring together the word families* of the following nouns:
(*A word family includes words of the same root formed by adding prefixes and suffixes. For example: love ➜ lover–lovely–beloved–loving–lovingly–lovebird...)

Person: _____
Joy: _____
Fear: _____
Truth: _____

Collect the rest of the sentences from the text with the verb 'have' and write them down in the space below:

1. She **had written** the letter to me shortly **before** she left this plane.
2. We **haven't seen** each other **for** several months now.
3. But I feel as if it **had been for** a very long time.
4. You asked me how I **had been**.
5. I**'ve been** okay except I miss you a lot.
6. I **have been** always **thinking** about you **since** you left.
7. _____
8. _____
9. _____
10. _____
11. _____

2. Sentence

The verb '**have**' is another important verb in English. It says that we own or possess something. For example: I **have** a car. My mentor **has** knowledge.

The verb **have** changes: have – having – had – had

Present Simple tense: I/You/We/They **have/don't have**…
She/He/It **has/doesn't have**…
Past Simple tense: I/You/She/He/It/We/They **had/didn't have**…
Future Simple tense: I/You/She/He/It/We/They **will have**/won't have…
Present Progressive tense: I **am having**/am not having…
You/We/They **are having**/aren't having…
She/He/It **is having**/isn't having…
Past Progressive tense: I/She/He/It **was having**/wasn't having…
You/We/They **were having**/weren't having…

Identify the tenses of the verb 'have' in the following sentences. Refer to the information in the box above if necessary:

1. My friend was having a great time. _____
2. They're having a meeting right now. _____
3. My boss has a lot of energy. _____

4. You have a rich experience. _____

5. I wasn't having my lunch at that time. _____

6. My parents had all my respect. _____

7. I will probably have a pet. _____

8. I'm having a headache. _____

9. My grandma is having her childhood friend over now. _____

10. You had no patience to wait. _____

The verb '**have**' helps form the **perfect** tenses.

How are the **Perfect** tenses formed?

Present Perfect: I/You/We/They **have**/haven't + **past participle** …
　　　　　　　　She/He/It **has**/hasn't + **past participle**…
Present Perfect Progressive: I/You/We/They **have been** + **present participle**
　　　　　　　　　　　　　　She/He/It **has been** + **present participle**…
Past Perfect: I/You/She/He/It/We/They **had**/hadn't + **past participle**…

---

1. The **Present Perfect** tense indicates that we have recently completed some action "perfectly."
   For example: I **have done** my homework.

2. The **Present Perfect Progressive** tense indicates that we have already started doing something but we haven't finished it (haven't "perfected" it yet), so we have to keep doing it.
   For example: I **have been doing** my homework since morning and I'm still doing it.

3. The **Past Perfect** tense indicates that we had completed some action in the past before or after something else that also happened in the past.
   For example: I **had done** my homework before my friend messaged me and asked for help.
   I **had done** my homework after my friend left.

Observe the use of the perfect tenses in the following conversations:

1. How have you been? I haven't seen you in ages.
   I've been okay. I've traveled a lot since I quit my last job.
   Oh, where have you been?
   I've been to many places.

2. Have you completed your studies?
   Yes, I have. I've been promoted to a leadership position, so I've been very busy since then.
   Congrats. Great to see you.
   Good to see you too.

3. Have you started a new project?
   No, I haven't. Not yet. I've been researching and analyzing the data for the project.

4. How long have you lived in this city?
   I've lived here for five years now and you know I've been living in the same apartment all this time.

5. Where have you gone for so long? I've been trying to reach you. What's happened?
   We had to take our grandpa to the ER. He'd tripped on the broken sidewalk and fell. His knee got injured very badly.
   Have you spoken to a doctor?
   Not yet. They've been performing surgery on grandpa's knee.

6. Where had you lived before you moved to Florida?
   I lived in California.
   Why have you moved to Florida?
   Oh, I retired.

Contractions: I haven't (have not); I've been (I have been); What's happened? (What has happened?); He'd tripped (He had tripped); They've (They have)

Complete the following sentences with the correct perfect forms of the verbs given in parentheses:

- The students _____ (pass) a difficult test with success.
- You _____ (not/see) our new neighbor, have you?
- My parents _____ (not/retire) yet.
- What _____ (do) since early morning? I _____ (paint).
- _____ (watch) that movie? Yes, I have.
- I _____ (never/be) to San Diego. I _____ (always/want) to visit it.

Make up sentences with the verb 'live' in the Present Perfect tense and the Past Perfect tense. Place them in the correct columns in this table:

Prior past	Past time	Recent past	Present time	Future time
	I lived in NY. I was living in NY all my life.	I've been living in NY for the past ten years.	I live in NY. I'm living in NY.	I will live in NY. I'll be living in NY for the next ten years.

Read this story about my friend. Then write a few sentences about your friend:

I have a good friend. I have known him since my childhood.

We didn't go to high school together, so we hadn't spent much time together until we got into the same college. He majored in psychology and I studied computer science. We hung out a lot during the college years. We had been hanging out a lot after college until I got married and moved to another city.

We're still in touch. He has already visited me several times over the past years. However, I haven't heard from him lately because he's been training for the next marathon. But I'm sure I'll hear from him soon.

Do you have a childhood friend? What is your story of friendship?

_____
_____
_____
_____
_____

Answer these questions:

- Had you done all the exercises before you reached this lesson?
- How much learning had you done by the time you got tired yesterday?
- What did you normally do after you had finished your studies for the day?
- Were you happy because you had bought this book?
- You hadn't studied English until you got this book, had you?

Note the adverbs and prepositions of time that assist in forming the perfect tenses:

Adverbs of time	Prepositions of time
already – yet	after (that time)
before – after	before (that time)
ever – never	for (a period of time)
eventually – finally	since (a point in time in the past)
lately – recently – by now – so far	from that time on
meanwhile	by the time
shortly before/after	as soon as
earlier – later	until
previously – beforehand	during
then – afterwards	while – after a while
just* (a moment ago)	within (a year) – in

(* In American English, the adverb 'just' is commonly used with the Past Simple tense. For example, I just emailed you.)

Choose from the options below or give your own answers to the following multiple choice questions:

1. Have you ever been to New York?
   a. I have never been to New York. (I haven't traveled to New York.)
   b. I haven't been to New York yet. (I haven't visited New York.)
   c. I haven't been to New York since last year.
   d. _____

2. Have you written the letter that I asked you to write?
   a. I just wrote it.
   b. I haven't been writing letters for years, so I'm not sure how to write them.
   c. I had already written the letter before you asked me to.
   d. _____

3. Had you researched the pros and cons of having that thing before you got it?
   a. Of course, I had.
   b. No, I hadn't. It didn't occur to me to do that.
   c. I always research things before I buy them.
   d. _____

3. Words

Demonstrative pronouns:

this—these; that—those ➔ demonstrate (indicate) the existence of something or someone

'**this**' refers to a singular noun that exists **near** us in space (and time)

'**that**' refers to a singular noun that exists **far** from us in space (and time)

'**these/those**' refer to plural nouns

Phrases:

there is/was/will be/has been—**there are**/were/will be/have been ➔ show the presence of someone or something somewhere in space (and time)

'**there is**' (there's) refers to a singular noun

'**there are**' refers to plural nouns

Look at the pictures and finish their descriptions:

This is a _____   These are _____   This is a _____   Those are _____

These are pretty _____   This is a nice _____   Those are little black _____

Name the things in the pictures below. Say where they are. For example:

There are paintings **on the wall**.   There is a painting **on an easel**.

(the piano/photos/bench)　　　(framed art/chair/pot)　　　(Xmas lights/gifts)

_____　　_____　　_____

Do the following:
- Look at your desk and name the objects that are on your desk.
- Look around your room and name the things you keep in there.
- Look out of the window and describe what you see out there.

Look at this picture. Determine whether the descriptions are true or false. Correct the wrong statements:

For example: This is a kitchen. → This isn't a kitchen. This is a dining room.

1. There is a desk there. _____
2. The dining table is by the window. _____
3. There are four chairs around the table. _____
4. There's a vase with flowers on the floor. _____
5. There's a rug under the dining table. _____
6. The coffee table is behind the couch. _____
7. There are two paintings on the wall. _____

Answer these questions about the place shown in the photo:

What is that?
It's a temple, isn't it?
What's in front of the temple?
What's behind the temple?
Are there trees around the temple?
What's next to the temple?

Describe the setting in this picture:

_____

_____

_____

_____

_____

Describe the scenery in this picture:

_____

_____

_____

_____

_____

Describe the situation in this picture:

_____

_____

_____

_____

Adverbs of place	Prepositions of place
Here – there Near/nearby – far Next door Inside – outside; indoors – outdoors Up – down; upstairs – downstairs Somewhere/nowhere/anywhere/elsewhere Right – left; to the right – to the left Above – below Toward – backward East – west – south – north...	at – next to – beside – by – near in – inside – within out/out of – outside on – upon – over – above – on top of under – beneath – below between – among behind – after in front of – before around – across through/from – to

Pronunciation:

- final stop consonants
- length of vowel sounds before voiced and voiceless consonants

1. Aspirated consonants: /p/–/b/; /t/–/d/; /k/–/g/ are **not** aspirated when they become stop sounds at the end of words. In the final positions, the air flow stops and they're usually not pronounced fully.
2. Vowels sound shorter before the voiceless consonants: /p/ /t/ /k/ /f/ /s/ /tʃ/ /θ/ but they sound longer before the voiced consonants: /b/ /d/ /g/ /v/ /z/ /dʒ/ /ð/. For example: speak–speed; bit–bid; bet–bed; back–bag

Read these sentences. Pronounce the stop sounds with <u>no</u> aspiration at the end of the words:

- This is a hat. That's a cat. Where's a cat? It's in a hat. There's a cat in a hat. But where's a hat?
- I like my bag. My bag is black. Do you like your bag? No, I don't.
- Where's my cup? I want soup in a cup. Look at a cup on a plate.
- Where's a park? I need to walk. Check on the map. It's up the street.
- Where's dad? He stepped out to get food. He'll be back in a minute.

Pronounce the vowels shorter before the voiceless consonants and longer before the voiced consonants in these pairs of words:

Advice–advise; badge–batch; cap–cab; cop–cob; lack–lag; log–lock; heed–heat; leave–leaf; grace–graze; teeth–teethe; pod–pot; mate–made

4. Sentence

Refer back to the mother's letter on page 107 and comment on these statements guided by the questions:

1. We haven't seen each other for several months now but I feel as if it had been for a very long time.
   a. Is a period of several months a very long time to you?
   b. Why did several months feel very long by an old mother?
2. You asked me how I had been. I've been okay except that I miss you a lot.
   a. In what circumstance will you ask someone how they have been?
   b. Do you think a person has been okay if they miss someone?
3. My life had been hard before you grew up and established yourself as a successful and intelligent person.
   a. Who is an example of a successful and intelligent person in your opinion?
   b. How do people establish themselves in life?
4. I have found peace and balance in my life and most importantly—fearlessness. Fear comes from the lack of knowledge.
   a. How do you imagine a life in peace and balance?
   b. What is the difference between a fearless and fearful person?
5. It's a little wisdom that a person has acquired with time and, as a parent, wants to share with their children.
   a. Is it true that a person has acquired wisdom with time?
   b. Why do parents tend to share their wisdom with their grown-up children?

5. Text

Write a few sentences to your dear one who you haven't seen in a while:

My dear...

_____

_____

_____

Yours,

...

Talk about the recent events in your life. Use the following questions to help you:

1. What have you done by now?
2. What have you done those things for?
3. Whom have you met lately?
4. How many people have you seen these days?
5. What places have you visited so far?
6. Where haven't you been yet?
7. How much money have you spent recently?
8. How much have you already saved?
9. What have you learned up to now?

Write a story about your recent dilemma. Mention which alternative you have chosen, how you have been making a decision, and why you have taken that decision:

I have recently faced a difficult choice./I've found myself in a tough situation...

Homework:
1. Seek out more information about the Perfect tenses.
2. Watch the online video titled: "Stop Sounds Overview–American English Pronunciation."

Lesson 10

Text: **On the Phone**
Present and past forms of the modal verbs: **can**, **may**, **must**
Phrases: be able/be allowed/have/need + to do; let/help/make + do
Modal adverbs and adjectives
Verbs of senses: look, smell, sound, feel, taste + adjective
Pronunciation: rhythm, thought groups, stressed and unstressed syllables, sentence stress, intonation

1. Text

"On the Phone"

This is a telephone conversation.

Jane: Hello. May I speak with Mary?
Mary: Hello. Do you mean Mary Walker?
Jane: Yes, that's correct.
Mary: This is she. Who's speaking?
Jane: Oh, hi Mary. This is Jane Miller. I'm calling to reschedule my appointment. I can't come this Friday as scheduled.
Mary: Okay. No problem. What date could you come over?
Jane: I could be there next Monday.
Mary: Let me check. Sorry but no time is available next Monday.
Jane: What about next Tuesday then?
Mary: Let me see. No luck for that Tuesday either. All is taken. But Wednesday looks good. Can you make it next Wednesday?
Jane: I think so.
Mary: Great. Can you come in the morning?
Jane: Morning sounds good to me. Can you take me at 10 am?
Mary: Yes, 10 am is good. Okay Jane. See you next Wednesday.
Jane: Thank you, Mary. Have a nice day.
Mary: Thanks. You too. Bye now.
Jane: Bye.

In the conversation, highlight the sentences with the modal verbs: may, can, could **and the sentences with the verbs**: look, sound.

2. Sentence

Modal verbs 'may, can, must' help describe possible or probable situations.
I/You/She/He/It/We/They **modal verb + verb**

Present tense: may, can, must

May ➔ permission, possibility, probability, suggestion, wish, or prohibition (may not)
      May I help you?
      It may rain tomorrow.
      May your dreams come true!
Can ➔ ability, permission, probability, possibility, request, or lack of ability (cannot)
      You can speak two languages.
      I can dance but I cannot (can't) sing.
      Can I use your pen?
      That can't be true.
      What can you do for me?
Must ➔ obligation, necessity, persuasion, possibility, belief, or impossibility (must not)
      I must go home. I must not (mustn't) be here.
      I must finish this work.
      What must I do here?

Observe the use of the present tense modal verbs in the following conversations:

1. May I come in?
   Sure. Come on in. How may I help you?

2. Excuse me. May I take this book?
   Yes, you may.
   Oh, I'm sorry. I believe you may not take this book.
   Which book may I take?
   You may take that one.

3. Can I use the restroom here?
   Yes, you can. Do you know where it is?
   Yes, I do.

4. Can you swim?
   Yes, I can./No, I can't.

5. You must be thirsty. Would you like a glass of water?
   Yes, please. I'd like some water.

6. You must know her, mustn't you? She must be your friend.
   I know her only as an acquaintance.

7. Must I take the test?
   Yes, you must. Thank you for your cooperation.

Past tense: might, could, must

Might ➔ suggestion, possibility, probability, or negative probability (might not)
    You might taste this hot cereal before offering. It might need more salt.
    You might like this book.
    You might not want to go there.
    It might snow.
Could ➔ ability in the past, possibility, permission, request, suggestion, inability in the past (could not)
    She could play the piano and the guitar.
    How could I help you?
    I could go with you, couldn't I?
    We could have lunch together.
'Must' ➔ used rarely in the past tense (instead: 'had to'), only with other verbs in the past tense (compound or complex sentences)
    I knew you must be busy.
    You thought I must have missed that opportunity.

Observe the use of the past tense modal verbs in the following conversations:

1. You might want to look at these instructions?
   Okay. Good point. Thank you.

2. Might they be on their way already?
   They might.

3. Excuse me. Could you please help me with filling out this form?
   I could try.

Give yes or no answers to the following questions:

- May I use your computer? _____
- Can I leave my bag with you? _____
- Must I take off my shoes to come in? _____
- Could I ask you to revise and sign this document? _____
- I might win the case, mightn't I? _____

Disagree with the following restrictions. Write the opposite versions:

1. You can't swim in a pool without a swim cap. _____
2. You mustn't wash your hands before eating. _____
3. Students may not hand in their term papers after the deadline. _____
   _____
4. We couldn't nap after lunch. _____
5. She might not try on her wedding dress until she buys it. _____
   _____

Fill in the blanks with the suitable modal verbs in the correct forms:

1. You _____ stop at the red light but you _____ walk at the green light.
2. We _____ speak loudly here. It's a public place.
3. My sister _____ run nonstop for an hour.
4. They _____ buy groceries yesterday but they didn't.
5. But they _____ stop by a supermarket today.

Explain to a visitor that the following is not allowed in the place of your work. Use polite forms of address in your statements: Mister/Mr., Miss (sir, ma'am /mæm/).

- Littering: _____
- Smoking: _____
- Driving: _____
- Diving: _____
- Criticising: _____

Answer these questions:

1. Why can't I fly like a bird?
2. Why can't I control the wind?

3. Why can't I hear wi-fi?
4. Why can't I see the air?
5. Why can't I taste poison?
6. Why can't I smell my ears?
7. Why can't I touch my mind?

3. Words

Other modal verbs:
- **should** → advice, recommendation, blame, reproach, regret
- **would** → wish (would like), request, invitation, usual action in the past

Substitutes to express permission, ability, and obligation:
- may → **be allowed to**
- can → **be able to**
- must → **have to, need to**

Read this golden rule in the different phrasing. Highlight the verbs: would, should.

Do to others as you would do to yourself.
We should do to others what we would expect others to do to us.
They should do to us what they would do to themselves.
That would make us good as we should be.

Play with the modal verbs: could, would, should. **Repeat them in such sentences as**: I would if I could but I should not.

I _____ if I _____ and I _____.
If I _____, I _____ but I _____.
I _____ and I _____ if I _____.

Advise what we should do in the following situations:

- We feel unwell. You should stay in and preferably in bed.
- We feel angry. _____
- We feel tired. _____
- We feel hopeless. _____
- We feel hungry. _____
- We feel restless. _____

124

Change these commands to polite requests. For example: Could you please...?

1. Call me at 5 o'clock! _____
2. Lower the volume. _____
3. Speak softly. _____
4. Help me with my homework. _____
5. Turn off the light. _____
6. Carry this box. _____
7. Make a copy of this document. _____

Insert the verbs could, would, **or** should **in these sentences**:

- The music is too loud. They _____ turn it down.
- I think we _____ solve the problem ourselves.
- Whenever we saw our family, we _____ spend time catching up.
- I _____ spend my precious time watching TV but I go out and walk instead.
- You _____ fall if you run fast. You _____ slow down.

Write the modal verbs for these substitutes:

1. The kids **have to** clean up after making a mess. _____
2. He **was able to** lift heavy weights when he was younger. _____
3. We **are allowed to** eat here. _____
4. A human being **is able to** discern what is good and what is bad. _____
5. We **don't need to** buy so much stuff for our small house. _____

Answer these questions:

- What are you able to do now that you couldn't do in the past?
- What do you have to do every day?
- What will you be able to do after you finish your studies?
- What is not allowed to do in your home?
- What do you need for your happiness?

Phrases:
- **would like someone to do something**
  I would like (I'd like) something/**to** do something
  I would like **you** to do something. I'd like you to do...
  I need + **to** do something./I want to do...
  I need **you** to do.../I want **you** to do...

- **let/help/make + do**

  Let me **do** this task. Let us (let's) do it together.

  This helps you understand this rule.

  They make us work overtime. (make someone do something = ask/cause/force someone to do something)

  Life circumstances make us change our thinking.

Observe the difference between these statements:

- I'd like a cup of coffee. I'd like you to get me a cup of coffee.
- I need to rest now. I need you to rest now and then resume work.
- I want to work on this project. I want you to work on this project.

Ask someone else to do the same. Write the next sentence:

1. I'd like to learn how to start a business. _____
2. I want to travel and see many places. _____
3. I need to visit our parents. _____

Highlight the phrases let/help/make someone/something + do **in the story below. Tell a story about your pet if you have one**.

"**Yoko**"

Meet my pet, Yoko. She's an example of freedom. She does whatever she wants. But as her owner, I guide her, well, to a certain extent. I let her do some things and don't let her do other things. I let her jump on my desk but I don't let her lick my laptop. I let her sleep in my lap when I am sitting but I don't let her sleep on my head or in my bed. Yoko is compassionate. She helps me fulfill my duties to her. She makes me buy her food and refill her bowl. She makes me clean her litter regularly. I make her behave well in the presence of my guests. When I have visitors, she is quiet. I appreciate her manners. I let her play noisily with her toys after the guests leave. She doesn't help me tidy up our home but it's okay. I forgive her for that because she gives me joy in other ways. One of them is the reminder that the symbol of freedom is present in my life. I also have a bunny, by the name of Leo, who is an example of quietude but I'll tell his story some other time… when Yoko and Leo become good friends.

Modal adjectives and adverbs:

- impossible, unnecessary, unlikely, likely, potential, possible, necessary
- impossibly, not necessarily, perhaps, maybe, possibly, apparently, clearly

Write the above adverbs on this scale by their degree of modality:

Low_____High

Change the modal adjectives to modal adverbs and write them in the table.

Adjectives	Adverbs
1. probable	1. _____
2. certain	2. _____
3. definite	3. _____
4. positive	4. _____
5. clear	5. _____
6. obvious	6. _____
7. total	7. _____
8. absolute	8. _____
9. complete	9. _____

Rearrange these statements by the degree of their probability from low to high:

1. I'm positive about that.   _____
2. I totally agree with you.   _____
3. I'm not sure whether he shows up.   _____
4. He'll probably visit us soon.   _____
5. It's completely wrong.   _____

Insert appropriate adverbs in the following contexts:

- My father is in a hurry. He's _____ late for a meeting.
- My friend is very responsible. He's never late. He'll _____ meet me at the airport on time.
- We'd like to have a fabulous vacation. Not _____ at the beach.
- My wife always goes to the gym at this time. She's _____ there right now.
- My husband is running late. He _____ got stuck in traffic.

Pronunciation:
- rhythm, thought groups, stressed and unstressed syllables
- sentence stress, intonation

Note: English is spoken with the rhythm timed by the stressed syllables. It means that only **stressed** syllables (words) are pronounced stronger and louder while unstressed syllables (words) are reduced and weak.
- Stressed words are content words: adjectives, nouns, verbs, and adverbs.
- Unstressed words are function words: articles, pronouns, helping verbs, prepositions, conjunctions, etc.
- Words are not separated when spoken. They're connected in thought groups. A thought group is a fragment of a sentence that gives one idea.

Read the folktale "The Sweet Soup Pot." First read it silently, then read it out loud. While reading it silently, **do the following**:
1. Highlight the stressed words in each sentence.
2. Separate the thought groups within the sentences with two vertical bars [||].
3. Show the rising intonation ⤴ wherever necessary.
4. Underscore the last stressed word in the sentence, which gives the sentence stress, and mark it with the falling intonation ⤵.

"The Sweet Soup Pot"

'Once upon a ⤴time || there was a 'poor 'little ⤴girl || who 'lived with her ⤵mother. They had ⤵nothing to 'eat. So the 'child went 'out into the 'forest || to 'pick some ⤵berries. There she 'met a 'good ⤴fairy || who 'knew the 'girl's di⤵stress. She gave her a pot with the power to give food. If one said to it, "Boil, little pot!" it would cook sweet soup; and when one said: "Stop, little pot!" it would immediately stop boiling. The little girl thanked the fairy and took the pot home to her mother. Since then they could have sweet soup as often as they wanted.

One day the little girl went out. In her absence, the mother felt hungry and asked the little pot to boil. The pot began to cook, and the mother ate all she wished. When she wanted the pot to stop cooking, she forgot what to say to the pot. Therefore, the pot boiled and boiled and boiled. The kitchen became full of sweet soup, then the house, and the next house, and soon the entire street. It seemed it wanted to satisfy the whole world so that nobody was hungry. At last, the girl returned and said: "Stop, little pot!" The pot immediately stopped boiling. But then whoever entered the village must eat their way through the soup.

4. Sentence

Observe the use of the <u>nouns</u> "chance, opportunity, possibility" **related to probability**:

1. I had the chance to express my opinion because I took the opportunity to speak.
2. We're all given opportunities to succeed but we often miss them.
3. There is a possibility of getting a new job and it's up to me to make it happen.
4. It was a good opportunity to change my career but I decided not to take it.
5. There is a chance (likelihood) that I'll have a business trip next month.
6. We may or may not face (have) the possibility of heavy snow tomorrow.
7. I just turned down the opportunity of working overseas, which I was offered, because I didn't want to be away from my family even for one day.

Finish these sentences:

- Once I had the chance of _____
- Last year, I had a possibility of _____
- Several years ago I passed the opportunity to _____
- I hope I will have a chance to apologize for _____
- My job had possibilities for _____
- There are many career opportunities in _____
- I need a chance to _____

Verbs of senses:
- seem, look, smell, sound, feel, taste + **adjective**

Observe the use of the sense verbs. Highlight the adjectives they are used with:

1. It seems late. We have to hit the road.
2. I'm glad she looks very happy today.
3. These flowers look beautiful and smell nice.
4. His new idea sounds great and it's likely we can accept it.
5. They feel tired after school. Let them rest for some time.
6. Your cookies taste delicious. Please tell me how you make them.

Fill in the blanks with the correct sense verbs:

- What are you cooking? It _____ good.
- You _____ fabulous in this dress.

- This fabric _____ so soft. It must be pure cotton.
- The cake _____ too sweet. I can't eat it.
- The lecturer's voice _____ pleasant.

Complete these sentences with the suitable adjectives:

- My mom's cookies always taste _____.
- Your idea sounds _____.
- Her father must be in a bad mood. He looks _____.
- Your new desk seems _____.

What would you say in the following situations?

- At the medical office, you'd like to ask their permission to use their phone to call your family because in a hurry you left your cell phone at home.

  _____

- At a job interview, you'd like to tell the interviewer about your qualities and skills.

  _____

- In class, you'd like to give your classmate a piece of advice about how to learn English more successfully.

  _____

- At work, you'd like to explain to your coworker how you would perform certain computer operations.

  _____

- At home, you'd like to assign household jobs to your family members.

  _____

5. Text

Message your boss and ask for permission to take a day off due to an emergency in your family. Explain the family situation and forward them your work agenda:

Choose to call your boss instead of messaging them. Imagine your conversation:

You: _____

Boss: _____

You: _____

Boss: _____

You: _____

Boss: _____

You: _____

Communicate your conversation with your boss to your spouse or friend:

Thank you!

Homework:
1. Look up information about the modal verbs, modal adjectives and adverbs.
2. Watch videos about the rhythm in English and practice it.

Celebration

In this section, you're going to celebrate your success. You'll review what you've learned in this book and witness how much English you now know.

1. Letters

Celebrate your knowledge of the English alphabet.

1. **Write the last letters of the alphabet, from "S" through "Z", in their order**:

   S_____Z

2. **Write the phonetic pronunciation of these letters**:

   "H" → /_____/; "w" → /_____/; "y" → /_____/; "z" → /_____/; "v" → /_____/
   "X" → /_____/; "g" → /____/; "j" → /_____/; "q" → /_____/; 'k" → /_____/; "r" → /___/

3. **Spell the following words**:

   Education, happiness, question, government, beautiful, awesome, downtown, important, delicious

4. **Think of more words that start with these letters and write them down**:

   "V": victory, _____
   "W": wonder, _____
   "Q": quiz, _____
   "Y": yesterday, _____
   "J": joy, _____
   "B": book, _____
   "R": request, _____

5. **Pick your favorite letters and write short poems about them**.
   For example:
   L is the light of the sun that fights the gloom of the room and lightens the days.
   O was an orange. It fell off the tree when it was ripe and ready for me to eat.

   _____
   _____
   _____

2. Sounds

Celebrate your English pronunciation.

1. **Pronounce these individual sounds**:

   Vowels: /ɝ/; /æ/; /ɑ/; /ɔ/
   Consonants: /w/; /h/; /ʃ/; /ŋ/; /t/; /r/; /l/

2. **Read these minimal pairs with the following sounds**:

   /i/—/ɪ/: beed—bid; seek—sick; seat—sit; deed—did; leave—live
   /ɑ/—/ɔ/: shot—short; sod—sword (the letter "w" is silent); cot—caught
   /u/—/ʊ/: food—foot; pool—pull; fool—full; wood—would; suit—soot

3. **Distinguish these words with the sound /ʊ/**:

   A cook　　　　a cooker　　　　cookies　　　　a cookie

4. **Compare the sounds /ð/ and /θ/ to other consonants**:

   Boat—both; thank—tank; tree—three; this—sis (sister); thing—sing; thick—sick
   Three—free; myth—miss; think—sink; sum—thumb (the letter "b" is silent)

5. **Read and memorize these fun tongue-twisters**:

   She sells seashells by the seashore.
   I scream, you scream, we all scream for ice cream.
   Peter Piper picked a peck of pickled peppers.
   A good cook could cook cookies as a good cook who could cook cookies.
   Lesser leather never weathered wetter weather better.

6. **Read this tongue twister with the correct rhythm**:

   Whether the weather be fine,
   Or whether the weather be not,

Whether the weather be cold,
Or whether the weather be hot,
We'll weather the weather
Whatever the weather,
Whether we like it or not!

7. **Read this verse of the children's song "Row, row, row your boat" with the proper intonation:**

Row, row, row your boat
Row, row, row your boat
Gently down the stream
Merrily, merrily, merrily, merrily
Life is but a dream

3. Words

Let's celebrate words!

1. **Name the things in the pictures. Use articles where necessary:**

_____   _____   _____   _____

2. **Name these occupations:**

A_____   a_____   a_____   a_____

3. **Identify the nouns by their definitions**:

A piece of clothing with long sleeves to be worn outdoors when it's cold.
A person whose occupation is to arrange and sell flowers.
A feeling when a person understands the misfortunes of others and helps.
An emotion when a person loses self-control and shows hostility.
A union of two people in the formally recognized relationship.

_____

(Answers: a marriage, a florist, a coat, anger, compassion)

4. **Write the opposites of these words**:

Single–_____; poor–_____; cheap–_____
Employment–_____; agreement–_____
Start–_____; enter–_____; remember–_____

5. **Think of synonyms for the following words**:

Pretty–_____; correct–_____; fast–_____
Opportunity–_____; gift–_____; beginning–_____
Select–_____; link–_____; achieve–_____

6. **Write the plural forms of these nouns**:

Parent–_____; child–_____; kid–_____; youth–_____
Woman–_____; man–_____; person–_____
Continent–_____; country–_____; neighborhood–_____

7. **Form the compound nouns by combining the following nouns. Remember to stress the first word when saying them**:

Air + craft = _____; bath + room = _____; boy + friend = _____
Class + mate = _____; eye + lid = _____; hall + way = _____
News + paper = _____; moon + light = _____
Sun + rise = _____; sun + set = _____; sun + shine = _____

8. **Form the nouns from the following verbs**:

Agree– _____; beautify– _____; create– _____

Decide– _____; mean– _____; simplify– _____
Succeed– _____; understand– _____

9. **Bring together the word families with these roots**:

Act: _____

Form: _____

Port: _____

Sun: _____

10. **Match the adjectives with the nouns they can describe**.

Adjectives	Nouns
Active	sunset
Cold	clothes
Loud	evening
Warm	voice
Romantic	fabric
Silk	music
Beautiful	weather

11. **Identify one word in each row that doesn't belong to the category**:

Activities: reading, fishing, amazing, praying, training, caregiving, filming
City: avenue, downtown, center, square, street, park, bicycle, building, road
Family: parents, siblings, strangers, niece, nephew, daughter, twins, toddler
Food: delicious, tasty, yummy, homemade, playful, healthy, colorful, beneficial
Nature: grass, lake, forest, river, tree, bush, furniture, mountain, valley, woods

12. **Guess the meanings of the underscored words in this context**:

I was born in 1975. I was raised by a single parent. We lived in a poor country where entrepreneurship was not encouraged. When I reached the age of ten, we managed to emigrate to another country where I grew up. I went to an engineering school and learned entrepreneurship. I had worked as a software developer at social media companies before I started my own tech company. We specialize in developing mobile apps for big corporations. We don't only provide services and fulfill orders but we also create our own products and sell them online.

Write the infinitives (base forms) and past tenses of the following past participles:

born _____

raised _____

encouraged _____

Write the meanings (translations) of these verbs from the context above:

to reach = _____

to emigrate = _____

to provide = _____

to fulfill = _____

to create = _____

Research and define the following concepts:

Entrepreneurship is _____

Social media is _____

Tech company is _____

Mobile apps are _____

4. Sentence

It's time to honor the sentence as a unit of speech.

1. **Insert the correct articles before the nouns**:

   - Let's have _____ birthday party. How many friends and family would you like to invite to _____ party?
   - We can meet at _____ restaurant around _____ corner. They serve great food. And _____ place is quiet.
   - I asked _____ manager about _____ upcoming business trip. She didn't know _____ details at _____ moment but she promised to give _____ answer within _____ week.

2. **Complete the sentences with the correct tense forms of the verbs given in parentheses**:

   - Look, it_____ (snow). I know. It _____(snow) since yesterday. Actually, it _____ (snow) all night long. And according to the weather forecast, it _____ (snow) tomorrow.

- I _____ (like) to garden. I _____ (enjoy) watching plants grow. Last summer I _____ (grow) vegetables in my backyard. It _____ (be) not easy but then I _____ (have) fresh vegetables till late fall. I _____ (think) of growing my own food next summer.
- Every time I _____ (visit) you, you _____(sleep). Last Sunday when I came at noon, you _____ (sleep).

3. **Correct these statements**:

   The sun rises in the west.
   There are 200 countries in the world.
   Money can buy everything.
   Ants have wings.
   The novel *Great Expectations* was written by Jack London.

4. **Enrich these sentences with the adjectives or the adverbs in parentheses**:

   You speak English _____. You speak _____ English. (good/well)
   You've learned English so _____. You're a _____ learner. (fast/fast)
   My boss is a _____ leader. She's _____ respected. (great/greatly)
   My sister paints _____. She paints _____ pictures. (beautiful/beautifully)
   His mom is a _____ person. She always treats him _____. (nice/nicely)

5. **Add the correct prepositions of time to these sentences**:

   It's been three days _____ we left home.
   We have been traveling _____ a month now.
   You shouldn't stay up _____ night and sleep _____ the day.
   I had been able to prepare dinner _____ my guests came.
   That happened many years _____.

6. **Add the correct prepositions of place to these sentences**:

   She used to live _____ Chicago.
   Her apartment was _____ the eleventh floor.
   She worked far _____ home, so she would get _____ work _____ bus.
   The bus stop was _____ the street she lived _____.
   So she could see people _____ the bus stop _____ the window.

7. **You're going to interview a person for a new job. Write down the questions you would like to ask them about their education and work experience**:

About their current job: _____

About the years of their work experience: _____

About their professional skills: _____

About their schooling and other training: _____

8. **Connect these simple sentences with the right conjunctions and form compound and/or complex sentences**:

My laptop is old and the operating system is outdated. I'm going to buy a new computer. _____

I love to travel. I get to know new places and cultures. I can't travel now. I have a small child. _____

You're now fluent in English. You have been studying it regularly and diligently.
_____

You need to start the journey. You want to achieve your goal. You know it.
_____

My dad would go to the gym every day. He was strong. He was also a man of willpower and self-discipline. _____

9. **Agree or disagree with these quotes. Explain why you agree or disagree**:

"Art is long. Life is short." ("Ars longa, vita brevis")
"A book is like a garden carried in the pocket." (Chinese proverb)
"As a man is, so he sees." (William Blake)
"Imagination is the eye of the soul." (Joseph Joubert)
"The sky is the daily bread of the eyes." (Ralph Waldo Emerson)
"Memory is the diary that we all carry with us." (Oscar Wilde)
"Love makes the time pass. Time makes love pass." (French proverb)

10. **Define the following concepts. Look at the provided quotes as examples**:

Art _____
        "Art is I, science is we." (Claude Bernard)
Music _____

"Music is the art of thinking with sounds." (Jules Combarieu)

Patience _____

"Patience is a bitter plant with a sweet fruit." (Old proverb)

Pen _____

"The pen is mightier than the sword." (Edward Bulver-Lytton)

Time _____

"Time is a great teacher that kills all its students." (Hector Berlioz)

11. **Read this story. Change the direct speech into indirect questions and answers. Retell this story to someone who needs to be more focused.**

"Arjuna's Focus"

There was an archery test in Dronacharya's gurukula (school). The guru asked his students to shoot an arrow into the eye of the made-up wooden bird placed high in the tree. He called the first student and asked him, "What do you see when you look up at the bird?" The student replied, "I see the bird on the branch behind the leaves." The teacher sent him back. Then he called another student and asked him the same question. The other student answered, "I see the sky, the tree, and the bird." He was not allowed to shoot, either. The teacher called Arjuna next. He asked him, "What do you see up there?" Arjuna said, "I only see the bird's eye, acharya." The teacher smiled and told Arjuna to shoot an arrow.

Arjuna was the best archer in the school. He practiced his archery skill even at night to be able to fight in the dark. Arjuna became an extraordinarily great warrior who later fought for righteousness.

- The teacher called the first student and asked him, "What do you see when you look up at the bird?"

  _____

- The student replied, "I see the bird on the branch behind the leaves."

  _____

- The other student answered, "I see the sky, the tree, and the bird."

  _____

- He asked Arjuna, "What do you see up there?"

  _____

- Arjuna replied, "I only see the bird's eye, acharya."

  _____

5. Text

Now celebrate your proficiency in English!

1. **Introduce yourself. Mention:**

    Your date of birth
    Your birthplace and a few details about it
    Your parents' occupations
    Your formal education
    Your work experience

2. **Give more details about your job. Use these questions as a blueprint for your talk:**

    - What kind of job do you do?
    - Why have you chosen your occupation (profession)?
    - What problems do you solve at work?
    - What do you help with: providing services or products?
    - What is your contribution to the company and humanity?
    - What work benefits do you enjoy?
    - How satisfied do you feel about your work, its outcome, and your income?

3. **Describe your achievements. Use these unfinished sentences as prompts:**

    I graduated from…
    I received an award in…
    I passed an exam in…
    I was certified as a…

4. **Speak about your family. Present each person in your family:**

    Your immediate family:
    - your grandparents (grandfather, grandmother)
    - your parents (father, mother)
    - your spouse (wife, husband)
    - your children (son, daughter)

    Your extended family:
    - your siblings (brother, sister)
    - uncles, aunts, cousins, nieces, nephews, etc.

5. **Check this recipe. Share it with your friend in the form of a story**:

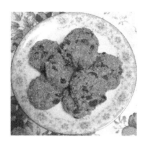

Flourless vegan chocolate chip cookies
Recipe type: dessert
Cuisine: American
Prep time: 10 min
Bake time: 15 min
Total time: 25 min

Ingredients:
1 tsp of baking soda
1 cup of grapefruit juice
1 tsp of cinnamon powder
a pinch of nutmeg
a pinch of cardamom
a pinch of clove
half a tsp of turmeric
1/2 cup of raisins
1/2 cup of cranberries
1 cup of toasted walnuts
2 cups of quick rolled oats
1/4 cup of melted coconut oil
1/4 cup of coconut sugar
1/4 cup of blanched almond meal
1/2 cup of vegan chocolate chips

Instructions:
- Drop baking soda in a mixing bowl, and pour grapefruit juice. Mix well till foam settles.
- Add spices, and stir the mixture.
- Wash raisins, cranberries, walnuts, and place them in the mixing bowl.
- Add rolled oats, coconut sugar, melted coconut oil, almond meal, and fold in vegan chocolate chips. Mix everything well.
- Heat the oven to 350°F (180°C).
- Prepare a parchment paper lined baking tray.
- Form cookies, and place them on the tray.
- Bake for 15 minutes.
- Enjoy your cookies.

6. **Describe the differences and similarities between this house and yours, between that room and yours**:

_____

_____

_____

_____

_____

_____

_____

7. **Speak about the valuable thing that is dear to you or your family. Use these questions to help you**:

What is it?
How did you get it?
Why is it dear to you?
What is it like?
What does this thing symbolize to you?

8. **Do the following**:

Give today's date.
Describe the current weather.
Describe the present-time season.
Give additional information about the general climate and usual weather in each season in your place of residence.

9. **Speak about your home country and hometown. Mention its**:

Location: _____
Population: _____

History: _____
Current economic situation: _____
Places of interest: _____

10. **Read this story. Decide whose New Year resolution you like most. Explain why. Speak about your own goal(s) for the next year:**

> **"At a New Year's Eve party"**
>
> At the New Year's Eve party, three guests started a conversation about their new year resolutions. One said, "Oh, I'm determined to get a well-paid job and buy a bigger house. I'll be having my fourth child next year." "Congrats!" the other person exclaimed, "But no children for me. I want to enjoy my life. Next year, I plan to travel more, taste different international cuisines, visit music festivals, and meet new people." "That's great! But I traveled a lot and found no big difference between there and here," said the third, "I realized, I need to stay put, still my mind, and find answers to many why-questions about my life."

I like _____ because _____
My New Year resolution is _____

11. **Talk about your daily schedule and activities. Describe:**

Your morning rituals
Your job routines
Your evening time

12. **Let's have a conversation about your love of English.**

"Do What You Love, Love What You Do"

You study English because you love to study it, don't you? It means you do what you love. That's fascinating!

However, you may find it hard to learn some things about English. You might feel discouraged and even pause your learning. In such a case, the other part of the wisdom comes into play: love what you do.

What does that mean? It means a change of attitude or mindset. For example, there are things in life that we don't love to do. What don't you like to do?

Maybe some household chores or work duties. But you have to perform those responsibilities anyway. However, if you keep doing those chores with a positive attitude, you will gradually start loving, or at least, appreciating them.

Let's say you feel overwhelmed by the complicated system of the English verbs. Can you speak without verbs? Rhetorical question! So the solution is to learn them anyway but with love. If you love them, they will love you back because they are also a vibration of energy. Then you both exchange loving energies.

What do you make of this idea: do what you love, and love what you do?

Repeat this wisdom in all verb tenses you learned and in all types of sentences:

Imperative sentence: Do what you love and love what you do!
Sentences in the past, present, and future tenses:

I _____

I _____

I _____

Sentences in the progressive and perfect tenses:
I am doing what I love and I am loving what I am doing.

_____

_____

_____

_____

13. **Take this questionnaire. Explain your choices**:

What is the most important verb tense in your opinion?
- Past simple
- Present simple
- Future simple
- Past progressive
- Present progressive
- Present perfect
- Present perfect progressive
- Past perfect

What is the most important period of time?
- Past

- Present
- Future

What is the most important part of the day?
- Morning
- Noon
- Afternoon
- Evening
- Night
- Midnight

What is the most important stage of life?
- Childhood
- Adolescence
- Youth
- Adulthood
- Old age

Who is the most important person in your life?
- President
- Mentor
- Teacher
- Doctor
- Grandparent
- Parent
- Sibling
- Spouse
- Child
- _____

What is the most important thing in the world?
- Air
- Beauty
- Compassion
- Family
- Fame
- Food
- Respect
- Strength
- Knowledge

- Money
- Love
- Work
- _____

What is the most important job?
- Administrative
- Artistic
- Caregiving
- Counseling
- Engineering
- Factory
- Teaching
- Medical
- Technology
- _____

14. **Share your perspective on furthering your English studies**:

_____
_____
_____

Congratulations on completing this workbook!

If you are reading this concluding part, it means you have successfully completed this workbook. It also means that you're fulfilling your dream of learning English. You aren't a beginner any more. You have graduated to the intermediate level.

This book has aimed at opening the door to the world of the English language for you. The ten lessons of the book provided an overall perspective of the language. Now you can continue deepening and amplifying your knowledge of English. If you need a refresher at any point, you can always come back to this book.

Continue your journey! Happy further English language studies!